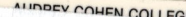

COLLEGE FOR HUMAN SERVICES
LIBRARY
345 HUDSON STREET
NEW YORK, N.Y. 10014

Competition, Cooperation, Efficiency, and Social Organization

ALSO BY Antonio Jorge:

Cuba and Canada: A Comparative Study (with Walter Frielingsdorf)

The Evolution of the Cuban Economy during the Fifties (contributing editor)

A Comparative Study of the Cuban and Puerto Rican Economies (contributing editor)

Some Aspects of the Relationship between Welfare Economics and Economic Development

Competition, Cooperation, Efficiency, and Social Organization

Introduction to a Political Economy

Antonio Jorge

Rutherford • Madison • Teaneck
Fairleigh Dickinson University Press
London: Associated University Presses

©1978 by Associated University Presses, Inc.

Associated University Presses, Inc.
Cranbury, New Jersey 08512

Associated University Presses
Magdalen House
136-148 Tooley Street
London SE1 2TT, England

Library of Congress Cataloging in Publication Data

Jorge, Antonio, 1931-
   Competition, cooperation, efficiency, and social organization.

   Bibliography: p.
   Includes index.
   1. Competition.   2. Cooperation.   3. Organization.
I. Title.
HD41.J66   1977   301.24   76-20272
ISBN 0-8386-2026-4

PRINTED IN THE UNITED STATES OF AMERICA

To my family
and all those who hope for a better future

Contents

Preface	9
Acknowledgments	11
Introduction: A Summary	13
1 Competition, Cooperation, and Human Nature in Society	19
2 The Internal and External Effects of Competition on Efficiency	34
3 Competitive Efficiency and Variations in the Organizations of Production	46
Notes	68
Bibliography	80
Subject Index	86
Index of Authors	88

Preface

This book is an abridged version of a larger project-in-the-making. It synthesizes in a social-science approach my thoughts on the subject of the relationship of various human and institutional elements in the protean field of competition and cooperation.

I believe, perhaps with the same trust in reason that Joseph Schumpeter attributed to the thought of the Middle Ages, that an objective network of human and technical interdependencies conducive to optimal results in terms of universally accepted final human ends exists in the realm of man's social life.

The weaving of objective and subjective factors at different levels of human action and in diverse facets of social life constitutes a structural necessity in any attempt to deal in an integral fashion with a perception of reality such as that described above. As indicated below in the introduction, the precise composition in the mix of these elements must be ascertained, utilizing the criterion of social and personal "utility," by the extent to which man's ultimate existential ends are realized by its operation. Therein resides, in terms of man himself, the true measure of the "scientific" character and value of the mix. Of course, cultural diversities will introduce, at a less abstract level of thought, the question of different but equivalent forms of social structuring and action.

The development of these thoughts is the agenda for which the present study is just a beginning.

Acknowledgments

I would like to express my appreciation to a learned former colleague of the faculty of Merrimack College, the Reverend Joseph A. Flaherty, for his valiant attempt to correct the grammar of this book while respecting its syntactical idiosyncrasy. I would also like to thank the Reverend Edward J. Burns for his encouragement and help in writing this book.

Introduction: A Summary

Competition and cooperation constitute antithetical approaches to human interaction. They represent the most basic general categories of motivations that are found in social life. Seldom, though, would we find them in pure form in real life. Rather, these two ingredients mix in an infinite variety of combinations, giving rise to a wide spectrum of different types of organizations. The skeletal or structural components of organizations will, in turn, reflect, particularly in the long run, the nature of the motivational composite operating in them. The nature of communication and decision-making, division of labor, and function coordination in the organizations will be strongly influenced by these motivations.

Competition and cooperation are to human behavior in society what supply and demand are to economic analysis — that is, broad classificatory categories that subsume large numbers of diverse individual factors under them. I submit that there is merit in analyzing economic systems in the light of these motivations. It will be shown that these motivations leave a clearly identifiable imprint in the composition and functioning of the categories.

It will also be found that there are several types of competitive and cooperative forms, each associated with different kinds of institutions and organizations. The main dichotomy will be between so-called competition and cooperation *with* and *for*. Each one of these signals a particular posture and is revealing of the social milieu and the culture in which it operates.

Some parts of the book are analytical, others descriptive, and still others prescriptive. A theoretical attempt is made to explain the actual patterns of economic behavior and existing organizational structures in terms of the logical concatenation that tends to develop between various levels of reality: philosophical thought, Weltanschauung, ideology, and motivations, among others. The objective is to show that these various layers are connected to one another and that a certain degree of congruity and integration is present in any given social situation. It also attempts to show that an important source of change in their relationships has its origin in inconsistencies and disconformities among the layers themselves.

The descriptive portion is concerned with a broad outline of a history of ideas in the sociopolitical realm in Western civilization. It purports to show the relationship between the evolution of political and economic ideology on the one hand and the nature of the institutional changes that have taken place in the Western European and American societies on the other. The role of religious ideas and their interpretation and application to social life occupy a central place in this section.

Finally, what may be called the prescriptive strand in this work consists in an effort to demonstrate that such concepts as maximal economic efficiency and productivity are culture bound. Economic optimization in the abstract is, to say the least, a not very useful concept. In any case, even to the extent that intertemporal and interspatial comparisons could be established, it can be demonstrated that there is no single institutional, organizational, or motivational path to attain optimization. The essence of productivity and efficiency can be incorporated into differing social arrangements.

The essential thing, though, is man's total development.

Introduction: A Summary

Economic systems must serve as a tool to that end and should not be viewed as ultimate realities in themselves. Economic efficiency must be blended with other variables necessary to human growth in a composite index whose value we should continually seek to maximize.

Historical explanation of the evolution of political, social, and economic concepts such as political authoritarianism and individualism, teleological economic objectivism and subjectivism, and objective social-class ordering versus subjective ordering — all are designed to convey an analytical understanding of the evolution of Western society in the light of this society's perception of some key concepts.

Competition and cooperation are the underlying and unifying themes in this work. Social, political, and economic structures are all ultimately characterized by a specific vision of the kind of relationships that exist or ideally should exist among the human agents that actuate them. This applies to collectivistic as well as to individualistic systems. Competitive and cooperative motivations transcend and transform formal organizational structures, regardless of how they came about historically. At the end, human motivations emerge, albeit gradually and laboriously, as the shaping force of history and social life.

It can be held that there exists an objective and realizable harmony between interdependent human and technological factors in society, which eventuates in a *maximum* situation as contemplated from the perspective of final, undisputed human ends.

The optimal social solution would require a complex interlocking of objective and subjective elements in the various areas of social life. The point is, though, that theoretically there is a unique solution for each cultural and historical situation, for the dual-faceted problem of structuring social behavior and organizational patterns in such a fashion as to maximize the realization of universally-agreed-upon final ends.

Looked at in terms of the attainment of these human ends,

each possible structural social pattern is subjected to the empirical test of social and personal "utility." Each proposed pattern of interacting behavior and structure must prove itself best in relation to all other patterns in the furthering of the stated final human ends.

Competition, Cooperation, Efficiency, and Social Organization

1
Competition, Cooperation, and Human Nature in Society

Cooperation, in the present context, necessitates goodwill, but does not require love in the sense of radical sacrifice. It is true that sustained and effective cooperation cannot be based solely on "enlightened egoism" and a detailed profit-and-loss calculation. In the end the two cannot be coextensive. If the two were to run parallel courses *ad infinitum* they would be, to all practical effects, indistinguishable. This is contrary to what I have called the "Divergence Principle."[1] Sustained and long-run, conscious cooperation, however, does require, under my possible assumption of goodwill as a motivating power, a belief in the overall harmony of individual and group interests. This belief, in turn, is central to economic sociology and in its main outline has traditionally been upheld by economic theory.[2] This, of course, does not preclude the harmonizing role played by the principle of the artificial identification of interests, originally held by Hume and

Bentham, nor the importance of the sympathetic fusion of interests, closely related to social structural issues basic to sociological theory. It should also be remarked that accounting for the existence of economic harmony does not require more than a mild degree of unconscious teleology.[3] An examination of the preceding clearly indicates the convenience of establishing a distinction between conscious cooperation and unconscious or unintended cooperation, that is, mere social coordination. The first one requires a measure of goodwill. The second is an unintended result of individual action and social processes. In the long run, though, if conscious cooperation is to endure without love or radical sacrifice as a motivating power, it must be apparent that "it pays." If there is conviction on the part of the individual that there is basic conflict or disharmony between him and the group, active or conscious cooperation of the type envisioned for continued development becomes impossible.[4] Now, at a more remote level, one can believe that cooperation is desirable either (1) because society should be organized and function in a given manner (ideological element of subjective ordering) or (2) because society requires it as a necessary condition of being (*Weltanschauung* itself as an element of objective ordering). Of course, the two can go very well together without any sharp distinction in the mind of a person. For example, society needs cooperation if it is going to survive, therefore it should be organized accordingly. Need and preference, however, may not go together. Although this should not be the case, society can keep on functioning in a conflictive fashion, according to the preferences of the subject.

From the preceding it is clear that one's attitude toward cooperation may be one of pure ideology, or entirely of *Weltanschauung* in its origin, or a mixture of both.[5] In turn, it may originate exclusively at this (these) level(s) or at a deeper philosophical one. A philosophical conviction about man, society, or the universe may lead to a given *Weltanschauung* and a practical attitude (at the praxeological level) toward cooperation. Yet there need not be a unifunctional relationship here. A conviction about man's weaknesses and imperfections does not necessarily deter those who hold it from striving mightily toward perfection, as they see it, in man and society.

A belief in the "nominal" or "fictional" theory of society, let me say, does not detract from the crusading spirit of old and modern-day liberals. A belief in the perdurability of the scarcity principle does not detract from the capacity of some to dream about unbounded improvement. Basic inclinations to regard man as aggressive or acquisitive do not impede the blueprints of utopia in their flow.

Cooperation may also be born from ultimate ethical positions or directly from philosophical explanations of man, society, and the universe, or, less articulately, from more immediate *Weltanschauungen* or ideologies, or, simply, at the end of the scale, from a temperamental preference. Although there are causal connections, even if frequently implicit and unconscious, from Philosophy (1) to *Weltanschauung* (2), from both to Ideology (3), and from all to Praxeology (4) and, furthermore, reverse causal chains making for a closed system of interaction, it is nonetheless true that for the purpose of immediate scientific analysis and manipulation (in constrast to general theories), we do well to concentrate on the proximate sources of action. That is, if we take an intermediate theoretical level (neither the general theory with its total, interrelated inclusiveness, nor a pragmatic and supposedly nontheoretical view) and a partial-analysis approach, we will be concentrating on the understanding and handling of individual situations existing at a moment in time, whose ultimate genesis and manifold ramifications are not, by far, so important as their immediate texture and cause.

Competition is the logical antithesis of cooperation, although the two may perfectly well coexist at different levels of action. Competition is a protean word that may be greatly confusing because of its utilization in a wide spectrum of different situations. In this context, the intent is solely to contrast the concept, in some respects, to that of *cooperation*. It would seem that a basic distinction could be drawn between being in competition *with* someone or *for* something on the one hand, and competition for economic and noneconomic goals on the other. Analysis of noneconomic competition must be altogether eschewed, of course, because the motivational assumptions it entails on the part of the economic agents in noncoercive situations are the opposite of those here utilized. Although competing *for* something always implies competing *with* someone — if there were prizes for everyone, it would not really, by definition, be any longer a competitive situation, except in the limit case of static, long-run equilibrium under pure competition — a distinction could still be made at the subjective level, which is, in this case, all-important. When the negative character of the competitive game is stressed, attention is directed to the interpersonal conflict created by competition. If such an attitude on the part of individuals becomes deeply ingrained and pervasive, coloring their *Weltanschauung* and/or idea of society, or — if one prefers to start at the opposite extreme — if their *Weltanschauung* and/or ideology were to condition their practical reason or praxeology in such a manner, it would serve to influence the tone of that society, even with marked independence of the nature of the economic institutions that characterize it at a moment in time. The inclinations and behavior of the members of society will help to shape the community in a distinctive form, even if a wide chasm such as that existing between market and nonmarket organizational forms were to separate two societies or, at the other pole, these psychological factors may establish distinctions between societies possessing similar economic institutions.

If, on the other hand, attention is directed at the goal to be reached competitively (e.g., in dynamic situations characterized by market expansion or by innovation), the element of personal antagonism is mollified. Now, it is important to realize that in the same manner in which competition *with* facilitates the appearance of a similar spirit in otherwise widely divergent societies, it is equally true that competition *for* has wide application in the very same types of antipodal societies.

The above leads to the conclusion that the nature or, if preferred, the spirit and goals of competition, may make a great difference in the quality and tone imparted to any society, regardless of the other organizational and institutional characteristics that define it.

The implications of this basic thought are many, and they find application in diverse areas. In relation to organizational theory, let me point out, it can be remarked that models are not completely determined in all aspects of their behavior by structural or mechanical conditions.[6] Lack of regard for this fact gives rise by a process of logical inversion to many crude versions of economic and technological determinism. The convergence hypothesis is one in vogue at the present time.[7] This is not to deny the high correlation and strong association that exists, *over the long run*, for *free and undisturbed* processes of interaction between human conduct and social institutions. But, by the same token, all kinds of short-run, culturally inconsistent developments, arising from natural or unique historical forces, often inject themselves into the workings of these processes. The subsequent dynamic between the social culture and institutions, between the individual and the environment, acquires infinite complexity and differentiates and redifferentiates itself indefinitely.[8]

It could be reasonably advanced that more of competition *for* is becoming increasingly necessary in contemporary market or mixed societies. As the mere size and great complexity of modern society increases, an orientation that focuses motivationally on personal distinction and achievement based on the attainment of social goals will be highly welcome.[9]

Competition *for* has the great advantage in modern society of underlining the existence and acceptance of social goals, even if these are to be attained in competition with others. No doubt this facilitates the blend of competition and cooperation. It is easier to enter into what may be termed convergent relations once it is established that this will serve a worthwhile social purpose.

The preceding may lead us to believe that the more we have of competition *for,* the better it will be for society. In my view, nothing could be farther from the truth. Competition *with* is also a highly essential ingredient of every economically progressive society. Again, one might suppose that even if this were to be so, the only reason for it would reside in the propensities and inclinations to be found, more or less strongly in the average individual, toward gain to be realized in competition, presumably at the expense of others (although in the equilibrium of the purely competitive model the expected result by each individual competitor — gain at the expense of others — never materializes), or because of the assertive and aggressive behavior exhibited by many individuals in their societal relations. In other words, one might be tempted to believe that, assuming the existence of an oppositely motivated society, competition *with* would not be needed for continued economic progress. The reality is that — even in the extreme theoretical case of an altruistic-disinterested utopia, where people would be actively predisposed out only toward cooperation, but even toward love and sacrifice — the fundamental problem raised by Friedrich Hayek for nonindividualistically organized economies, that of the impossibility of concentrating in centralizing bodies the amount and kinds of knowledge necessary to make the right economic decision at every instant for every possible situation, would remain with us.[10] Notice that this is inevitable insofar as the absence of competition *with* forces economic functions into one large cooperative whole or unit for each type or kind of function. That is, to the extent that people are unwilling to compete *with* one another, they must then discharge the function in question in a purely cooperative fashion. It follows that a very high degree of control and planning will eventuate from such a situation.

This holds true, of course, even assuming that the trusts or combines that would result from the agglomeration of firms in each industry would enjoy perfect freedom. Of course, if they are not going to engage in competition for economic resources against one another, or grow lax in the absence of internal prodding for efficiency, or if buyers (consumers and producers) will not try to maximize, there is no sense in which we can speak of a competitive (efficient) price system. On the other hand, dealing with questions of economic efficiency would be much diminished in such a society. Seeking efficiency would tend to take place in a physical-technological sense rather than in what would tend to be the alien context of purely economic considerations.

Naturally, the further that we relax the assumed condition of an altruistic-disinterested utopia, the more difficulties we will experience in trying to sustain economic progress without competition *with*. Ultimately, and at the polar opposite of our utopia, lies the nightmare of a fully collectivized and perfectly centralized economy, apparently dreadful even to the Soviet and similar regimes (although with still some well-known abdurate adherents), if we are to judge by the efforts to increase efficiency on the part of Stalin's successors. This is, without this type of competition, and under the possible range of actual conditions in the real world, we will end up with the worst characteristics of collectivization and centralized decision-making. Competition *with* is necessary to make for economic efficiency and to facilitate growth in resource productivity.[11] All of this is, of course, within the traditional province of economics. But the role of competition *with* as a fundamental building block in the field of political institutions merits equal consideration. The relationship of the concept to the institution of private property and to the question of the state powers and their degree of concentration or diffusion is a *locus classicus*. The modern group of writers who call themselves libertarians have elaborated on this matter at great length.[12]

Naturally, competition *with* labors under the traditional disadvantage of not being glamorous. Even worse, it seems to be downright disagreeable to many people.[13] Even if in some people's eyes it were to be greedy, we have the very realistic consolation pointed out by Lord Keynes when he said that it is better for people to tyrannize their bank accounts than others. Even then he suggested that the monetary prizes earned in the game could be cut in size without an impairment of efficiency. Perhaps one could take the events of the last few decades in the fiscal field as a confirmation of this belief in the developed societies of the West. But the central fact not to be lost sight of is a rather different one. The elimination of competition *with* in society would not, by any means, even in the quasi-limit case of the altruistic-disinterested society, eliminate the potentially dangerous motivational nub inspiring competitive behavior, namely; the self-directed, maximizing syndrome in the individual. On the contrary, the suppression of that outlet would only channel such forces as the desire for distinction, possessions, or power, along with the aggressive behavior propelling them, into definitely more baneful directions for society and the individual.

It would seem that anthropological and modern historical evidence would tend to confirm that socially enforced pseudo-harmonious institutions that unduly constrain individual expression, or do not allow for it in relatively harmless forms and areas, will force such expression into finding outlets in the most diverse manners and fields, ranging from external aggression at one extreme to savage intra-party politics and an unresponsive and domineering bureaucracy at the other.[14] Sports, incidentally, will not do as a substitute. Not everyone has the requisite abilities or inclination or, for that matter, is willing to settle for that kind of a prize. Incidentally, there is no derogation or moral defect in this. On the contrary, many able and idealistic persons, to mention just one category of candidates, will always aspire and be ready to fill positions of power and influence in society. This is fortunate, insofar as it is not possible to organize and run society as a paradigm of the olympic games.

The foregoing raises a twofold question, the first concerning the relations of the psychic forces and goals identified with the maximizing syndrome to the basic traits of the human condition. Again, as in the case of an individual's motivations, the economist *qua* economist, has to avoid direct involvement with the field of philosophical anthropology or psychology. Nonetheless, one must squarely confront, on a purely empirical and phenomenological basis, the question of the manifestation of these traits in observed human behavior. Without going into the study of ultimate causes (reductionistic approach), or without trying to pry into the actual mechanisms that would *explain* human behavior by resolving it into some kind of a model (mechanistic approach), we constantly assert our capacity to understand human beings and human action in the study of the humanities and of history. Much more important, we use that knowledge in everyday social intercourse and living, and also in all spheres and levels of thought and action. Furthermore, we engage in all kinds of predictions with regard to the malleability, possible transformations, and derivations of human nature every time we plan or provoke change in the cultural, social, political, or economic fields.[15]

At the intermediate (*Weltanschauung*-Ideology) level at which political economy moves, we need not claim more specific or scientific knowledge of human nature than that resulting from perceiving or grasping the meaning of human actions as behaviorally observed and as interpreted within the framework of some intermediate-level, theoretical notions about man *qua* individual and *qua* social being. No social science that would not be completely sterile and that aspires to more than formal validity can, in principle, deny this. The economist can avoid many such complexities, as is generally admitted, to the extent that he deals with concrete and specific, so-called economic problems, within a set of given institutions and assumed modes of behavior. Nonetheless, even in the realm of economic policy in advanced countries, seldom can the economist venture out on his own with any high assurance of attaining desired results.[16] This, of course, is not new. In economics there has always been present, although in varying contexts, the preoccupation about the legitimacy and true extent of the claims put forth by the science. Increased meaningfulness and application would require traveling between the Scylla of Scientism and Radical Positivism and the Charybdis proposed by German Idealism and the Old Historical School.[17] Now, the maximizing syndrome would withstand the test of its reality or existence at any of the four specified levels of thought and action of man in society: Philosophies (1); *Weltanschauungen* (2); Ideologies (3); Practical Reason (4). The confirmation of its operation may be negative, that is, by way of the desire to change some of the more concrete and immediate results or manifestations of the syndrome as they appear in one cultural context or the other. But in any case the reality of the armature or receptacle that contains the basic drives and forces producing such effects is acknowledged by both those who approve and those who disapprove of this or that set of actions flowing from its operation.

It should be noticed in passing that the maximizing syndrome does not presuppose or in any manner imply psychological or ethical hedonism. As a matter of fact, it just assumes rationality of conduct with a view to the attainment of given goals. Economics, in that sense, would constitute, as has often been stated, a particular application to social reality of the wider category of actions termed rational or intelligent. It is also increasingly recognized that maximization is not a type of conduct exclusively confined to modern man. Instrumental rationality of action at a given level of technology — be it in the economic field as such or, as may be the case in many nonliterate cultures, the will to maximize in a wider social context — seems to be a universal in human culture.[18]

We might say that, ultimately, man is a purposeful animal. Man uses his undifferentiated psychic energy (the *libido* of Carl Jung) to attain goals. That is all that needs to be postulated for the present level of discussion to be meaningful.[19]

The second question is related to the limits of the malleability of the basic human structure. Again we confront one of those fundamental and monumental questions that have been asked in many different forms and contexts, without ever receiving a definite answer. It is safe to affirm that no definitive answer will ever be forthcoming, because there is no solution to this manifold query that subsumes all of the facets of man and may itself be posed in an almost infinite number of ways and contexts. In order to exemplify this, let me pose the analogical problem of precisely what constitutes excessive coercion, limitation, or regimentation of human social action and expression, and how this coercion affects human conduct and development, and, in turn, how all of this reflects and impinges upon other areas of human thought and action. This riddle is probably at bottom a way to verbalize the innumerable, different combinations of variables and their values (political systems, social milieus, economic institutions, child training, personality formation, and the like) that would define each possible, specific, human situation of that nature. No two functions would be identical and no two answers would be the same. Paradoxically, it is equally as true to state that we cannot postulate, even less solve such riddles, and thus quantify our answers, as it is to say that the human intellect is quite capable — through its capacity to abstract and generalize as to the direction of the resultant in the vector field of social forces, and through the process of induction based on historical material — of giving reasonable, logically sound, and qualitatively demonstrable answers that would serve to demarcate the contours of the areas of possibility involved.[20]

There is no real difficulty in understanding and even predicting human conduct, under specified social models, as a statistical average. Naturally, predictions in the social sciences in the real world are not accurate, simply because the complexity of reality far surpasses that of any operational model.[21] Of course, it need not be said that if at an ultimate philosophical and ontological level we believe human beings to be possessed of freedom, then any prediction, no matter if based on the most complete model, may fail to materialize.[22] We may paradoxically repeat with the astrologist: "The stars influence but do not determine."[23]

All great economists — nay, more — all great social scientists with a specialized training in economics have worried about the effect of social structures and institutions on man's nature.[24] Karl Marx may have been the first to refer specifically to alienation, but the concern with the dehumanization caused by repetitive tasks was born with Adam Smith. The very preoccupation of classicists and neoclassicists with the stationary state reveals their concern with the impact upon man and society of changing economic conditions. We see this tradition carried into our own day in the works of John Maynard Keynes, John M. Clark, Frank H. Knight, John Kenneth Galbraith, and Kenneth Boulding, among others, not to mention the main corpus of institutionalist thought. It is interesting to find at present a psychoanalyst with the perspective of an Erich Fromm warning us that man is not infinitely malleable, that he can adapt only so far to organizational structures before they begin to dehumanize him. Man is not all kaleidoscopic change and adjustment to buffeting forces. Below many changeable layers there is a hard core to be reckoned with.[25]

Of course, there is a vast difference between postulating limits to social pressure and manipulation on the one hand, and the preservation of mental health on the other, and the legitimate attempt at selecting optimal social institutions that, within permissible limits of variation, will fit different historical realities. In the concrete case of Fromm, there is an undiluted preference for social forms involving conscious cooperation which, in my opinion, is not objectively validated by the established requirements of human nature or by the need-satisfaction and goals sought after by man in society. The next chapter to some extent touches upon the related question of cooperation and conflict.

It is worthwhile to notice that, at least in the tradition of the more general thinkers in the social sciences, there has not to my knowledge, developed, a position holding the complete plasticity of the human mind. The concept of limits in the range of variability, or at least of increasing difficulties and of ensuing undesirable results when the magnitudes and rates of change acquire certain values, underlies the historical contributions in this area. Cultural anthropology and social psychology are the fields that can best illustrate this.

This position on the other hand seems to be denied, even if implicitly, by the modern totalitarianisms. Marxism, of course, by upholding the socially derived character of man's consciousness, takes an explicit position on this crucial question. This undoubtedly allows totalitarian systems to embark on ruthless social experiments and manipulation of the individual with, supposedly, a theoretical justification for it.

In the end, the substratum of competition and the root that nourishes its varied manifestations reside in the phenomenon of power.[26] Even if one succeeds in molding people to accept the practice of competition *for,* making them more goal-and society-conscious, more mindful of the need for cooperation, the fact is that the better qualified are going to compete for the right to grant the medals, that is, for the positions of prestige, power, and leadership. Aggressive tendencies — dominating tendencies — are going to keep on surfacing under the most varied disguises. Even those who behead in the name of equality are unequal. Robespierrean terror was the prerogative of the Jacobins, just as Mao Tse-tung's drive for the creation of an immaculate machine (the new man) was conducted by a small minority.[27] In the "limit" situation, for the "evil" effects of competition to disappear altogether one would need a psychological attitude based on the following paradox: the only recompense or satisfaction to be reaped by engaging in socially beneficial action is that of experiencing complete and total self-disinterestedness in the act of serving others. Short of that state, competition will always express itself as a form of power. The elements of domination, superiority, assertiveness, the elation of victory, or the sensation of having overcome others in its many-faceted manifestations, are the logical counterpart of disinterestedness and service for service sake.[28]

Now, one may subscribe in varying degrees to a well-known line of thought on "basic" human nature epitomized by Ashley Montagu's little book *On Being Human* (New York: Hawthorn Books, 1966), without drawing the socioeconomic conclusions that to some seem to follow inevitably from it.

So, to say that "human nature is oriented in its primary thrust toward goodness. Human *nature* is good. It is human *nurture* that is bad" (p. 121), or that "man is born for cooperation, not for competition or conflict. This is a basic discovery of modern science" (p. 109), does not necessarily indicate that there is an antithesis between the "Christian ethic of love in relation to the business ethic of competition of 'free enterprise,' for example" (p. 101). This reflects a partial view of man in society rather than a complex and holistic one based on the weighing and meshing of man's various needs and aspirations and their translation into roles and structures.[29]

Moreover, the anthropological evidence does not seem to indicate the existence of any Golden Age in either nonliterate cultures or rural life in Western civilization. Mental disorders and psychosomatic illness, as well as warfare and crime, are universal.

Excessive reliance on the naturalness and spontaneity of conscious and freely given cooperation under certain social conditions gradually glides into the various shades of collectivist and communist anarchism, with their emphasis on unlimited mutual cooperation and aid among the members of the commune. In practice these ideas of course lead straightforwardly to political violence.[30] The reality of human nature is not that conceived by anarchism nor that which many early anthropologists thought they saw in nonliterate cultures.

The case for the total elimination of competition and egoism and their manifestations on biological, psychological, political, social, economic, or ethical grounds remains to be established.[31]

Now that this has been said, the important thing is both to comment on the attainable blends of competition and cooperation under given conditions of time and space, and also, if possible, to point out which could be, again under various constellations of circumstances, the possible mixtures or blends that may historically arise in the future of mankind.

2
The Internal and External Effects of Competition on Efficiency

As has been previously indicated, conscious cooperation does not require love or the capacity for radical sacrifice, but only goodwill among the participants. It is true that cooperation must be based on a belief that certain goals, important enough so that partial renunciations and accommodations will be accepted by the individuals in society, can be realized only by common action and concerted effort. But it is also true that, without a measure of goodwill supplementing the pure intelligence and comprehension of proximate ends and means, it is practically impossible to surmount all of the obstacles and accept all of the sacrifices that sustained or institutionalized cooperation demands.[1]

This is expressed in the social science literature of our times in a variety of ways. By way of illustration, in the terminology of David Riesman, the concept of *otherliness* conveys the notion of an awareness and sensitivity to our medium that is a characteristic of modernity, even if filtered and restricted in outlook to the dimensions of our peers' perspective. In the case of Talcott Parsons the pattern variable of *collectivity-orientation* signifies a concern with interests other than our immediate or personal ones. It stands for an orientation toward society and others.

Also, Kalman Silvert, among other political scientists concerned with the phenomena of modernity, notes how modern man must display in his socioeconomic behavior certain predictable characteristic that will enable him to establish secure relations with others.[2] One could take this to be a mollified version of the Weber-Sombart-Tawney spirit of rationality permeating advanced societies. Parson's pattern variables exemplify the contemporary sociological expression of the behavioral requisites of modernization.

Although these are all different concepts devised by their authors for specific application in widely different contexts, there is nonetheless a relatedness among them. They all imply a degree of dissociation in the individual from a myopic, narrow, or extremely immediate view of his interests. There are nonetheless always potential gains, at least in the short run and for some individuals, in noncooperation.

It was because of the lack of goodwill in his state of nature — *bellum omnium contra omnes* — that Hobbes conceived in *The Leviathan* of an absolutist state as being needed to restrain the unbridled utilitarian desires of antagonistic parties to maximize their gains. In his *Two Treatises of Civil Government,* Locke, on the contrary, sees a more beneficent human nature typified in reasonable individuals who mutually respect their natural rights and socially cooperate for purposes of long-run (constrained) individual maximization.

The classical sociological tradition in economics, by contrast, hails from the Lockean view of harmony and convergence of interests in social cooperation through division of labor. In this model, competition in a pure market provides most of the checks necessary on the agents' self-interest (and, according to Malthus, on excessive population), and a mild government supplies an appropriate economic framework besides ensuring against fraud and violence.[3]

With all of this in mind, voluntary restraints are, to say the least, always doubtful. On the other hand, state regulation, which seems to be the logical solution, is not really a restraint, but only the easy way out. Coercion is the antithesis of cooperation, and it leads, if not carefully controlled, to all of the undesirable results with which we are so familiar.[4] Ultimately, coercion not only is conducive to disastrous political and social results, but also does not even succeed as an organizing and stimulating agent in the technical economic field.

Competition, on the other hand, is by no means to be eliminated as a motivational force. Cooperation in and of itself would, most probably, be insufficient for a healthy sociopolitical and economic order.[5] It is clear that even the "limit" case of the altruistic-disinterested utopia would exhibit an important technical flaw. It would be connected with the great difficulty of arriving at an efficient price system for goods and services in the *necessarily* centralized decision-making milieu that noncompetitive forms of organization would bring about.[6] Besides, as has been frequently argued, competition is necessary for a variety of other reasons: to preserve the identity of the smaller social units (individuals, family, voluntary associations); to allow them to express their preferences and individuality; to permit them to strive for the maximization of their well-being; to help preserve their political freedom; and, last, to allow these organizations to lead a less-than-ideal (perfect and irenic brotherhood) and arcadian life, but one closer to the characteristics of average human behavior.[7] There are many possible mixes of cooperation and competition and these will vary according to time and place. Such mixes, by their very nature, must be made with a view of satisfying many different types of human goals and values which, in turn, exhibit considerable differences at the cultural and individual level besides being subject to transformations of their own.

If the foregoing is true for the narrow economic case, it will be so *a fortiori* if we conceive of the competitive-cooperative mix as being also directed at maximizing the long-run rate of economic growth by helping to create favorable noneconomic conditions for this purpose.

Reverting again to an analysis of the fundamentals of competition, we could conceive of its demise in the other-directed utopia under the following two situations: (1) that in which all but one individual would renounce pursuing their well-being by subjecting themselves to a sociopolitical and economic minimization at the hands of the sole unconstrained maximizer in these fields, possibly because of compensation in another sphere of being,[8] and (2) a community of identically minded individuals, in which there would be no disagreements concerning the operation of production, distribution, and consumption activities. Again, this situation would be impossible in practice — such a unanimity not being in accord with the diversity of human views, valuations, and preferences — unless the consensus were to arise from the subsidiarity of these goals and their subservience, as pure instrumental means, to more highly valued ends shared by all the members of the community. In such a case, then commonly accepted, probably egalitarian rules governing economic functions would become established.

Given the fact that human society does not conform to these two exceptions and that, in part, our interest in the competitive question resides in the investigation of the relationships existing among various possible organizational patterns of economic activity and their compatibility with competitive behavior and economic efficiency, let us then ask what lines of thought may be suggestive of tentative answers.

The first point to recall is that the individual is the only substantive maximizing unit recognized in the field of economic analysis. The second is that only the purely competitive model succeeds in defining structural and institutional, including behavioral, conditions and relations such that every individual participant will end up maximizing his gains, subject to a constraint consisting in everybody else's doing the same thing. In order for this to be the case, the model provides for a solution according to which the return to each unit of every factor will be in accordance with the marginal value-productivity of the factor in question. This view, which considers society as a conglomerate of income receivers, is that of functional distribution in the economic field. Other marginal conditions ensure maximization — again subject to the constraint of the existence of more than one unit — as viewed from the standpoint of the exchangers, be they producers or consumers. It is to be noted that the maximum of aggregate satisfaction that this model yields — under the mentioned constraints — results from the acceptance of two conditions: (1) the equality of all individuals in their capacity or, at least, in their formal right, to acquire economic gain leading to the experiencing of utility, and (2) equal diminishing marginal utility of gains for all or, barring this, their formal right, again independently of the slope of the curve, to obtain economic gain.[9] In order to explain the actual case of observed divergences among individuals and their sharing of utility, it can always be argued, for both (1) and (2), on the basis of a basically identical human nature and assuming the existence of appropriate socioeconomic policies, that present dissimilarities will eventually disappear through the creation of future homogeneous environmental conditions. This, in essence, has always been the position of orthodox economics, derived from the acceptance of the classic and neoclassic tenets of political economy (in the sense of moral philosophy) regarding human nature and social change.[10]

The third point to be recalled is that the mutual interaction of all units of the economic agents involved in the game succeeds in *leveling the amount of power* possessed and exercised by each and every participating unit.[11] This is what makes possible, in the last instance, the appropriation by each unit of an amount of value equivalent to its contribution, as rated in the market by all concerned.[12] The fourth element to remember is that both the optimal size of plant and combination of resources in the equilibrium situation flow automatically as a consequence of market competition itself. That is, they are shaped or forced into their final form by external pressures that oblige the surviving firms to go in that direction. It should be noticed that this applies to all aspects of the structure of the firm: production, management, finances, markets, and the like. Diseconomies of scale at both ends of the spectrum are eliminated by the operation of the automatic and relentless mechanism of competition.

With the above points in mind, it could perhaps be suggested that the double effect of competition as an agency for individual welfare maximization and as a motivational stimulus to effort arises from the following fundamental fact: the construction of the competitive model is such that, in spite of the inevitable aggregation and conglomeration of people in socioeconomic units dictated by social cooperation under the principles of division of labor and specialization, and to a certain degree in conformity with the existing technology, still each unit of every economic agent can and does act in pursuit of its own welfare. All the units are free, and they exercise their freedom directly, that is, without mediation, in the prosecution of their own ends.[13] The units act by and for themselves within the complex of organizational shells (structures) in which they are integrated. Aside from all the individual or personal requirements that are necessary if this type of behavior is to be effective, still other kinds of socioeconomic institutional and organizational conditions are necessitated if the units are to express themselves individually. These can be basically reduced to the existence, as an end product, of *perfect mobility for the units along a continuum of open alternatives for action at their disposal.*[14] This is what ultimately allows the agents to act in their own behalf with decisiveness and celerity, bringing about the results anticipated by the model. It is in this accommodation of conditions, behavior, and desired effects that what we may call the *internal* efficiency of competition lies — that is, the efficiency that hails from the type of human behavior made possible by the structural and relational conditions defined in the model.[15] In contrast to this internal efficiency we have the element of *external* efficiency, deriving from the optimal conditions of plant and resource combinations (including types and degree of complexity of intramanagerial and labor-managerial relations), which flow from the efforts of the individual firm to survive and prosper despite the external pressures brought against it by all the other firms in the industry. The *external* efficiency effect, therefore, depends on the double condition of optimal size and factor mix (optimal absolute and relative resource combinations) and in the reciprocal checking and restraining of firms. As a matter of fact, optimality itself results from the actions characterizing the process of mutual restraint.

Now, regarding the manner in which other organizational forms or structures different from those of the classic and neoclassic economic models could be fitted into the wider institutional framework of society in such a way as to preserve the operation of both the internal and external effects, the basic thought could be advanced that the essential factor to keep in mind in attempting this incorporation is that of preserving the substance, again in contrast to the mere forms, of the competitive arrangement.

In brief, the solution lies in providing ample room for maneuver or freedom of action for the individual (no matter how he specifically happens to be grouped or socialized), and also in maintaining sufficient external pressure against each separate grouping of individuals or producing unit. The latter is simply obtained by avoiding as far as possible any form of monopolization or concentration of economic power in the hands of any single unit. It is important in this connection to avoid local monopolies, government privileges that are granted to certain types of organizations and denied to others, overt or tacit collusion among the units, and the like. If enough competition is preserved among all the units regardless of their different types or kinds of organizational forms, not only will external efficiency become strengthened, but the internal aspects of it as well. By preserving the possibility of substitution among factors and their units, fostered through fluidity and openness, we ensure that the social conditions for freedom of individual action will obtain.

All this would be required, of course, even if the single object of policy were to consist exclusively in furthering economic efficiency — which anyway is never the case in fact. From a more realistic standpoint, and if one wants to introduce cultural considerations into a more encompassing social welfare function, it would be perfectly possible to distribute handicaps through public policies so as to preempt undesirable organizational results of unfettered competition. Paradoxically, it may be that such an approach will in the long run succeed in creating such economically favorable human conditions in the productive units that the productivity of labor and the type and efficiency of managerial relations in hybridized market firms will surpass the maximal efficiency of a culturally bound competitive model. It would be worthwhile, and highly important in the context of promoting economic development, to investigate the conditions under which a short-run, second-best economic policy is conducive to a long-run, *maximum maximorum* situation.

As a last point, it is probably desirable to maintain alternative types of economic organizations, not only in order to foster freedom of action within the same society, but also to avoid a possible form of universal or blanket inefficiency extending to all units in the system. This could result from overcomplexity of management, such as indecisiveness in decision-making processes, tardiness in effective action, and related evils deriving from excessive meddling of owner-managers in, say, production cooperatives. The requirements of efficiency should be preserved against undue encroachment by anarchistic participation in decision-making.[16] After all, the hierarchical character of decision-making in complex (above the single individual level) social units is an unavoidable, functional fact of life. But inefficiency, on the other hand, is not the exclusive privilege of exaggeration or deformation in that direction. Extremely centralized, rigidly hierarchical, oligarchic, or simply mechanistic, uncreative, and ahuman forms of organization, inside as well as outside the confines of the productive units, could lead to similar results.[17]

Turning now to the unresolved issue of group satisfaction in contrast to classical individual-utility experiencing — typical cases of which are to be found in the field of family life everywhere and also where collectivity rather than individually oriented economic activities exist — this constitutes a completely different problem. There is no doubt that such situations will have somehow to be increasingly incorporated into the study of modern economies.

Theoretically, the problem exists and would apply in principle in the case of all forms of cooperative production and consumption in what we consider to be modern societies, as well as in nonmarket and nonbalanced reciprocity distribution patterns among so-called primitive, preliterate, or illiterate peoples. Let it be said in passing that there is an abundant literature on this last point in the field of economic anthropology, but although it is seemingly applicable to our query, there are substantive differences to be considered. The general belief in the communally oriented character of some aspects of life in many of these cultures in contrast to modern ones brings us to the heart of the difficulty. Yet the closest, to my knowledge, that anthropologists have come to a consideration of this question is when they insist as, say, Karl Polany and George Dalton do, that the economic sector in preliterate societies is an interrelated part of the community's life that cannot be meaningfully extricated or separated from the whole. No doubt, once the economic function is seen as the source of satisfaction of other than economic needs, we shall have made some progress in realizing the complexity of the issue. But economists have also admitted that much when they insist that economic phenomena are but a means for the realization of the most diverse ends. Joseph Schumpeter, Friedrich Hayek, and Frank H. Knight, among others, have certainly coped with this issue explicitly. But I am dealing here with yet another aspect of group action in modern societies that is not limited either to traditional methodological or definitional disputes in economics or to the universal or relative aspects of culture in archaic or subsistence societies — namely, with the impossibility of apportioning among participating individuals the total economic utility generated by collectivities (collective units) in situations where they function not only as the relevant unit of economic action but also as the ultimate recipient or beneficiary of that action.

The problem of decomposing aggregate or social values into individual ones would be a process the opposite of determining the social value of something, or its value to society. This is a question that has vexed economists for a long time and for which a completely satisfactory and universally accepted solution seems improbable. Although collectivities are composed of individuals, if the latter cannot be assured of the existence of associational alternatives and perfect mobility, then there can be no definitive or clear way of ascertaining the net effect on individual economic welfare of intra-group changes provoked by collective action. This conclusion is of course based on the standard assumption made at present in economics regarding the impossibility of ascertaining the cardinal utilities of individuals and, *a fortiori*, of establishing interpersonal comparisons of utility among them.[18]

Nonetheless, collective satisfaction will have to be given more recognition in the field of technical economics. How can this necessity be reconciled with the fact that groups are not persons, but only aggregations of them, and that there is no way in which one can go about attributing to the group a will of its own? The common welfare or public good is partially dependent on the welfare of aggregates that act in a unitary fashion. We deal with these aggregates in practice and cannot ignore their existence in our analytic considerations.

This problem is not exclusively restricted to economics and the notion of the social welfare or utility function, but arises also in the context of the goals and functions of social organizations and again in the political concept of the public interest. No doubt the twin risks of the reification of society and of its goals on the one hand, and the denial of their existence as separate entities on the other are always present. Ultimately, we may find antagonistic philosophical positions underlying the divergences in this field. Strong idealistic and empiricist stands can hardly be reconciled in their perceptions of social reality.[19]

The best and at the same time perhaps the only realistic and practical manner of wrestling with the complex issue of individual and collective satisfaction, at least from an economic-welfare standpoint, is to assume — given, of course, the necessary conditions — that the groups are *freely made and sustained associations of individuals, having the capacity, means, and opportunity to withdraw from existing groups and form still others, or to remain unattached as individuals if they so desire.* Therefore, the groups are, under the assumed conditions, surrogates for the individuals constituting them. In this particular light, we will perceive no difference between the competitive Smithian or, more to the point, Marshallian firm and other, less conventional groups.[20] After all, the difference may be simply one of size. The classical or Marshallian firms are represented as being small, but certainly they are not coextensive with their single owner. As a matter of fact, any production unit composed of more than one individual would present in essence the same problem. This is as true of hunting-gathering bands as it is of extended families in traditional societies, and as it would be of cooperatively discharged labor. It would seem that the existence of freedom in the form of readily and abundantly available alternatives open to the individual holds the key to the solution of our problems. If this is so, the notions of competition and of external and internal efficiency may still be made useful to the study of nonconventional (from the standpoint of orthodox analytic economics) forms of economic organization.

3
Competitive Efficiency and Variations in the Organization of Production

I can only briefly outline here a question that may well constitute one of the central topics of any realistic study of modern institutional economic forms. It could be posed as follows: Can the essence of the purely competitive model become incorporated in social and economic forms other than that of a conglomerate of atomistically dispersed producers? That is, is it possible to obtain the maximizing results of the purely competitive model with an organizational pattern that would embody its content or substance but not its form? No doubt the purely competitive model is the historical and analytic foundation on which economic theory rests. Such has been the case since Adam Smith and John Stuart Mill, assessed the situation in equivalent terms at the beginning and at the end, respectively, of the classical period.[1] In this same context it is interesting to notice by way of illustration how in our own time Jan Tinbergen, in discussing the question of the optimum regime in planning, remains within the bounds of neoclassical economic theory.[2]

Because the sociopolitical panorama has experienced profound changes since the close of the classical and neoclassical periods, it is not surprising that the problem of the substantive relationship between economic efficiency and institutional forms should come to the fore again. A good contemporary example in the literature of the urgency for such an inquiry is the challenge posed by the socioorganizational implications raised by John Kenneth Galbraith's concept of countervailing power.[3]

It is interesting to note how at present a new political economy exhibiting a more organized and cooperative or group-directed view of social action, in contrast to the highly individualistic and atomistic view of classical political economy, serves to introduce what may eventually become a Trojan horse for economic theory. It is true that the notion of counterpoise and balance may also be introduced via the less suggestive and more technical road of oligopoly. In effect, certain kinds of oligopolies, endowed with the appropriate characteristics, may yield results not too far off those of the competitive model.[4] In effect, the Galbraithian thesis takes the concept of oligopoly as its starting theoretical notion, and in doing so remains within the traditional bounds of economics (if the study of "imperfect" forms of competition, and of market forms other than perfect competition and monopoly may, indeed, be labeled *traditional*) but, of course, the difference lies in the application and implications that Galbraith squeezes from his construction. These are definitely no longer in the customary province of economic theory, traditional or otherwise. George Stigler has very effectively criticized the Galbraithian construction from a technoeconomic standpoint precisely because it is simply not amenable to the tools of economic analysis. No empirically verifiable inference can come out of it, nor is it possible for rigorous economic analysis to rest on it.[5] Nonetheless, the urgency of the issue of relevancy does not disappear because of our invocation of the inability of the tools at our disposal to resolve existing problems. It seems that we shall have to find a way to deal, even if approximately and defectively at first – and possibly also by means of an interdisciplinary approach – with the theoretical aspects of the intra-cooperative behavior of producers grouped in single units of action or decision-making. We shall also have to find a way to deal with the related question of the consequences of the competitive behavior of these units among themselves.

The similarities and dissimilarities between the structure and behavior of the competitive firm of traditional economic theory and cooperative-participative forms of organization will have to be closely observed with a view to discovering whatever general relations, tendencies, or associations exist or may come to exist between efficiency and other-than-purely-competitive organizational models. One would be inclined to believe, *prima facie*, that the efforts of practically all of the branches of the study of man, but most particularly the behavioral sciences, will be necessary in the search for a realistic answer, in contrast to a purely conditional and speculative treatment of this matter. Many of the branches and methods of modern business administration and of the study of human behavior in general would find ample room for application in this area. The study of human relations, the administrative sciences, and organizational theory in general would be very helpful in elucidating the fundamental questions and in setting up the theoretical skeleton basic to handling the problems involved. Among the most important points whose investigation is essential and that readily suggest themselves is the firm's size. As is well known, the size of the producer under pure competition is specified only relatively to the extent of the market, and not in absolute terms. Because of real-life situations one tends naturally to think of

Competitive Efficiency

such firms as being typified by the family farm or the small enterprise owned and managed by the individual proprietor. But this need not be the case. The beneficial effects flowing from competition are ultimately derived in large part from the checking and counterbalancing forces brought to bear by each firm upon all others. That is why we can conceive of some oligopolies and monopolistic competitors coming as close in their market behavior to the competitive industries as is technically possible for them to do. This result flows from what I have termed the *external* effect of competition. There is, though, a second result, which also flows from the same effect. It boils down to the fact that competition forces the surviving firms to adopt the optimal plant size for the production of the good in question while at the same time it standardizes a situation of minimal cost and maximum efficiency in resource use. Now, optimal plant size varies extensively from one industry to the other. It is frequently large enough to render invalid the traditional notion of the small firm directly managed by its single owner. In those circumstances, as is often the case, although the firm's efficiency may in part be still dependent upon the outside prodding of competition by rival firms producing an identical product or a close substitute, the resulting situation, in terms of the firm's size relative to the market for the industry, is such as no longer to allow us to speak of pure competition as materializing.

The main conclusion to be derived from the preceding is that in many cases, and well before we find diseconomies of scale (decreasing returns to scale) — due according to many experts to the impossibility of indefinitely and proportionately extending equally efficient management *pari passu* with the other factors — the functions of management in the owner-supervised and directed firm will have grown in complexity greatly beyond what is required of them or would be conceivable. The modern enterprise in many branches of industry clearly exemplifies this situation. The various layers of management, with their elaborate vertical ordering, hierarchical communication, and intricate decision-making processes, administering in the name of a diffuse host of stockholders, may well often be the paragon of efficiency, but they certainly do not fit the notion of the purely competitive model. Such structures, by the very nature of the case, exhibit a high degree of internal coordination and cooperation. Furthermore, the cooperative trait is a necessary condition of efficiency in those cases. This, of course, is at the core of what the administrative sciences are concerned with, and could hardly be new to a student of management or organization, especially if he happens to be interested in the literature on competitive and cooperative attitudes and behavior, the nature of leadership, and the types of relationship in the management of the modern firm. Nonetheless, such a triviality may be worth emphasizing. It may very well be — and this, again, by now constitutes the bread and butter of the "managerial-society" strand of literature — that the managers will maximize in accordance with a composite of their own, different from the short-run monetary-profit index preferred by the "lone wolf." This in itself is no objection. Such maximization, independently of whether we like it or not or approve or disapprove of it, is the result of a given ordering of preferences on the part of the decision-makers.[6]

In reality, the difficulty raised by different forms of cooperation is of another nature, namely, that posed by the likelihood of some relationship existing between efficiency and the *direct* participation of owners (stockholders), in various conceivable forms, in the actual production and managerial functions of a cooperative venture. In other words, in what way, if any, is management in a corporation different from the type of management to be expected in a cooperatively owned venture directed by, or under, the direct supervision and the more-or-less immediate and detailed participation of the owner-producers? It would seem on the face of it that the greater the direct and immediate or detailed participative and decision-making power of those other than the purely functional and organizational managerial cadres in charge of the technical and operational direction of the firm, the greater the overall inefficiency of the process. Workers' councils, wherever they have been in charge, are a good example of this.[7]

The reasons for such an outcome are almost self-evident, ranging in nature from ignorance, confusion, and delays to politicking and inhibited management. The twin principles of authority and participation in cooperation coexist in modern firms but, we should note, with the following restrictions: (1) deliberations are circumscribed within the managerial ranks and do not extend to workers, (2) management is essentially hierarchically organized[8] and therefore can ultimately adopt and enforce decisions, and (3) participation does not override, as a matter of right, specific technical competences and responsibilities of the firm's officials.[9] Even with the operation of these provisos the managerial factor, as noted above, cannot expand indefinitely. Increasing factors according to scale or in strict proportion causes insuperable difficulties in the fields of administration and decision-making. These arise mainly because the nature of the relations among managerial ranks varies of necessity as they increase in complexity and also because the capacity of the human mind itself to cope under optimal conditions with a growing number of simultaneous relations does certainly decrease from a given point onward.[10]

Naturally, these difficulties will be compounded to the extent that the technical restrictions upon participation are weakened. It is not possible to define *a priori* the optimal degree of complexity for the managerial network under varying sets of conditions or for different types of organizations. The finding of the solution for each particular case would automatically follow from the operation of the external effect of competition, if it were allowed to work freely and evenly throughout the economy. But, on the other hand, it is clear that if participative conditions of a given sort are to be imposed upon production establishments as necessary organizational traits, then we should expect that only by accident will there be a coincidence between optimal organization and the postulated degree of participation. Of course, one realizes that there are many possible degrees and forms of participation. Partaking in the direction and administration of economic processes is a multidimensional function capable of being defined in many ways and subject, within limits, to implementation in specific areas and under many different conditions.

Perfect participation, in the sense of individual involvement in each decision and action, is manifestly impossible. Considerations of economic efficiency and even physical limitations imposed by the requirements of production itself will restrain participation much before it could in any sense approximate the "limit" value of perfect involvement.[11]

We do not expect total participation on the part of the stockholder-owners of modern corporations, nor would we expect it to be the ideal of the populist variant of capitalism. No one would make that a necessary condition for full economic and social responsibility and involvement, even for the "limit" case of diffusion of ownership throughout the entire population and assuming the required knowledge, alertness, and interest of all in both personal and social affairs.

This being the case, it can more readily be perceived that the forms and degrees of participation may vary quite substantially from one milieu to the other without any necessary implications following in regard to the *quality* of the population, even as measured by some objective and commonly accepted standards of social modernity. Such criteria as level of formal education, involvement in political affairs, volume of intake of various types of information, and the like, do not point to any single solution to this question.

Ultimately, the patterns of involvement in managerial and decision-making processes will substantially depend upon each culture's definition of the size of the relevant unit of participation, decision-making, and control in production and social activities in general. It is quite possible to expect, in the dynamics of cultural change, enculturation, and cross-cultural fertilization, many alterations and hybridizations of these patterns. It does not seem necessary to assume, or even to regard as probable, any kind of standardization with regard to forms or degree of participation based on an implicit universalization of the Western or, specifically, the American culture patterns. These, in turn, are themselves open to further evolution and change, if only because of the dynamics exhibited by the institutions and values of American society.[12]

We should not always expect to find clearly formalized patterns of participation at every historical juncture for every society. In actual practice, participation will probably avail itself of many informal and circuitous channels and multifarious forms in expressing itself. Improvisation and stochastic historical occurrences will also contribute, in all probability, to the creation of many unexpected variants in participative modes.

It should also be noted that no specification of formal relations in an organizational model can cover the range of behavioral nuances introduced by the presence of varying and often imponderable elements, like the personality traits of participants or the singular cultural forms of a society.[13]

Another factor to take into consideration is that, although informal structures are not completely independent of the formal ones, there is always room for divergence. Consider the following quotations: "The fact that an organization has been formally established . . . does not mean that all activities and interactions of its members conform strictly to the official blueprint." And "The constituent groups of the organization, like all groups, develop their own practices, values, norms, and social relations as their members live and work together."[14]

Nothing could better exemplify this than the wide range of concrete results that accompany the functioning of cooperatives, depending on the conditions prevailing at their inception and the actual motivations and goals of the participants.[15]

Besides, given that cultures are not logical constructs exhibiting perfect consistency, we can also expect considerable deviation, especially under dynamic conditions of change and progress, in the molding and patterning of involvement and participation. This is desirable insofar as it will serve as a constant prod to the attainment of a higher level of economic efficiency through the fostering of the external effect of competition. An outlet for the exercise of the latter is provided by the coexistence of diverse organizational patterns open to all social aggregates ranging from the single individual upward to the large corporation.[16]

It should be noted that the working of the external effect of competition need not lead to the organizational standardization of production. Although in principle it is probably true that in a purely mechanical sense, as noted elsewhere, maximum economic efficiency for any given activity is dependent upon a determinate set of conditions that will give the advantage to one market form over the others, still this is so only in a very restricted sense. It is equally probable that even economic efficiency, not to mention the fulfillment of other essential individual and social goals, may reach successively higher maxima under organizational forms differing from the apparently optimal one. The explanation resides in the different "spirits" of the organizational modes. The attitudes and behavior of the participants are fundamental independent variables which, in conjunction with the varying structural characteristics of alternative modes, will produce a wide range of values for each activity. Not only will the prevailing animus have a marked direct influence on producers, singly or collectively considered, but its very real effects on possible organizational forms and types of managerial relations, as well as on their effectiveness, will also be decisive.

The structural characteristics of organizational modes themselves will possess different degrees of effectiveness according to the cultural milieu in which they are called to function. No society has ever rationally and consistently tried to optimize economic efficiency "single-valuedly." Therefore it cannot be simplistically claimed that a given form of economic organization that is especially congruent with a particular culture is efficient in an absolute and universal sense.

This is not to deny the obvious fact that some cultures have been more dedicated than others to the pursuit of economic values and more determined to mold themselves in accordance with the supposed, abstract requirements of economic efficiency. But we cannot judge by their success the value of other cultural alternatives. This is especially so because the remarkable proficiency of some cultures is mainly attributable to the role played by the increase of scientific knowledge and its technical application to production through both human and nonhuman inputs.

The rationalization of production organizations and their contribution to efficiency, on the other hand, cannot be evaluated in terms of any existent, or even theoretically formulated absolute standard. It would be manifestly absurd to counter this by affirming that Western culture has patterned all of its culture and its institutions in an optimal response to the single goal of economic efficiency. If we admit this to be the case, then it must be confessed that we are just ignorant of what possible mixes of technology and human attitudes, behavior, and institutions would, *in abstracto* and independently of particular cultural settings, absolutely maximize economic efficiency. When we observe modern technology mixed with a "backward" human factor in an underdeveloped country, we know we must "modernize" the latter if we are to have a higher degree of economic efficiency. Unfortunately, our present knowledge is not sufficient to determine what efficiency values may be attached either to the performance of labor under various organizational alternatives or to the managerial and organizational forms that would result from the presence of different "spirits" in the human beings involved.

Are we to believe then that the overall organizational shell or framework of competition to which I have been attributing such great merits can be dispensed with, perhaps at no cost at all in efficiency? This would not seem to be a valid conclusion. The internal and external effects of competition are extremely important in fostering efficiency. However, we should not confuse these effects or aspects — which, flowing from a given set of socioeconomic conditions and corresponding types of human attitudes and behavior, serve to define and delimit the competitive case — with the concrete and specific morphology or structure of the organizations that have been brought about by the working of these effects or aspects. Competition has to be disembodied, so to speak. We have to separate the conditions that make competition possible from the actual shells or forms that will make these conditions operational. It would be perfectly possible, then, to have if not identical, at least nearly equiefficient but organizationally different productive forms of association. The external effect of competition itself would help to pressure the varying forms of organization into an acceptable efficiency range.

Aside from these considerations, public policy may be used in manifold ways in a conscious effort to promote a situation of near equiefficiency. In this connection and because of the alternative approaches to policy it opens, it is worthwhile to emphasize that the causal chain in the genesis of

Competitive Efficiency

competitive market forms need not inexorably run from (1) outward institutional conditions, like the industry's conglomerate of atomistic optimal firms to (2) logically congruent (rational) forms of economic behavior, which (3) produce the attitude or spirit identified with competition. The actual sequence could be just the opposite. Let us briefly consider these two possible courses of development.

The Weber-Tawney-Sombart (psychological or cultural) approach to competition relies on a behavioral propensity that does not hail, as in the previous sequence, from outward institutional conditions that generate its existence. It rather consists in a "spirit," whose presence and prevalence in various cultures and times have been the topic of many works in economics, sociology, and anthropology. My interest at this point resides in calling attention to the competitivelike market effects of such an animus, regardless of the specific organizational forms on which it happens to operate.

It should be noted that the competitive results do not stem from a countervailing-power type of theory. Their explanation is not based on the notion of competing bilateral oligopolies producing competitive results. All that needs to be assumed in a general fashion is that the nature of the market *Weltanschauung* will be a competitive and not a collusive one. In other words, the presence of competition is explained as a culture trait. Finally, the unquestioned existence of that type of behavior would not make the producer's actions any less rational than those of its collusive counterpart. The optimal solution for the individual producer must always be contemplated within a given, initial frame of reference. Economic rationality cannot be expected to anticipate and quantify the long-term results of opposite courses of action based on sociologically and psychologically radically different alternatives. After all, in the course of events we accept society and ourselves as given background for the purpose of shaping our actions. If this were not the case, a revolution would have to precede every one of our acts.

The competitive spirit — one might dare to say the *acquisitive* spirit, both being totally coextensive in the purely economic sphere of activity, eschewing differentiating marginal connotations — would give us a perfect example of the competition *with* concept discussed above.

All that need be asserted here is the widespread existence of this type of economic behavior, not how it came about or in what respects, if any, it differs from its counterpart in past epochs. There does not seem to be any disagreement, once the question is posed in terms of factual ascertainment, that economic aggressiveness, as a manifestation of the unshackled acquisitive spirit, is a distinguishing trait of the so-called pure capitalistic system. Max Weber, after describing the *ethos* of rational but traditionalistic business, shows how the arrival of dynamic entrepreneurs changed the whole situation even without any essential change in the form of organization. As he puts it: "The idyllic state collapsed under the pressure of a bitter competitive struggle."[17] Likewise Tawney tells us that the "acquisitiveness which cannot rest while there are competitors to be conquered or profits to be won . . ." was converted into moral virtues that had once been cleansed in the waters of Puritanism.[18] Also Dempsey, commenting on Sombart's *spirit of competition*, which the latter believed was a typical feature of capitalism, writes the following: "Competition was different in the nineteenth century than it was before. The elder Toynbee indeed defined the so-called Industrial Revolution as nothing more or less than the market changes resultant upon the abolition of the market control exercised by the guilds. The competitive situation, heightened by improved transport and communication in both internal and foreign markets after the passing of the guilds, might indeed furnish grounds for calling the modern economic era the Competitive Society. . . ."[19]

Finally, the old attitude exemplified by "competition is the life of trade" can be usefully contrasted to the effects of the modern spread of the stock company and the concentration of control in the hands of relatively small minorities.[20]

The working of competition *with* would definitely tend, to the extent that technical constraints would allow this, to bring about the competitive results that the purely competitive model has familiarized us with. Following this line of thought, it would be possible speculatively to run an opposite, but logically symmetrical exercise to my previous one concerning institutional competition, by just inverting the hypothetical genesis of market forms. Given the proper conditions, we could then end up with an equilibrium situation under pure competition generated, *ab ovo*, by the action of a competitive spirit working upon a reality amenable to transmutation in that direction. These time-honored logicohistorical exercises, though, are noted for their futility. There is no actual way in which the chicken-egg riddle can be disjointed and regressed to time zero or origin. Thus, we cannot ascertain which came first, the "spirit" or the institution.

Actually, this does not affect our present pursuit. We are not interested in the logical identity and outcomes of historically dissimilar sequential processes. It is more productive to notice from a pragmatic standpoint that, within probably not-too-wide margins of tolerance, acceptably similar competitive effects could be obtained from two coexisting but widely different socioeconomic market structures. This is perfectly possible, in principle, for many a different market configuration. Given the adequate conditions, an oligopolistic variant need not be, as to its economic effects, distantly removed from the results that would obtain for the same industry under a formally "purer" model of competition. Monopolistic competition or the Chamberlinian group may, in other instances, approach other types of oligopoly in the imperfection of its performance.[21]

I am not discussing here, of course, "limit" situations, which by the nature of the case cannot ever produce identical results. It is impossible, say, to reach equilibrium at the minimum point of the average total-cost curve except under pure competition. But refinements such as this cannot realistically constitute a goal of policy-making, especially in underdeveloped countries. Policy instruments in underdeveloped countries are, generally speaking, crudely applied and managed. If this were not so, the problem of increasing economic efficiency would be much more tractable to the coarse policy instruments at the disposal of underdeveloped countries than experience shows us to be the case. Another costly casualty of inefficiency is a much-needed program directed at promoting workable competition in the markets of these nations.

There is, I hope, no contradiction here beween the organizational morphology of markets and the acceptance for many oligopolistic situations of the well-known mutual-dependence notion. Moreover, the existence of the oligopolistic category and the recognition of the importance of further search for determinate solutions in this field do not contradict the existence, under certain circumstances, of competitive (aggressive) behavior in the marketplace. More important, it becomes self-evident and almost tautological that, as we advance in the continuum of market forms toward situations characterized by facility of entry and a correspondingly larger number of firms in the industry, this aggressive behavior becomes increasingly more likely to occur. Therefore, although the direct and indirect effects of an oligopolist's actions, and the sharing of profits by the members of the industry with or without common agreement are standard features of oligopolistic theory, other factors and constellations of circumstances must also be taken into consideration.[22] Among these, quality competition, advertising, and the problems of free exit and entry into the market are important.[23]

An interesting quotation relevant to the question of the possibility of divergence in oligopolists' perception of their role expectations is provided by Fellner: "The problem of the degree of competition is essentially a problem of how close (substitutionally) a firm's products are to those of other firms, and how *independently* the individual firms behave in

Competitive Efficiency

the market structure".[24] He then adds: "If the market structure contains oligopolistic traits, in addition to product differentiation, then this gives the firms much greater control over the price than does product differentiation alone, *provided the oligopolistic firms act concertedly.*"[25] In relation to this, one could ask if the familiar historical instances of cutthroat competition and expansionist leadership in large industries in American economic history were not a reflection, partly at least, of deeply ingrained competitive attitudes. It would probably have been impossible, in the light of such a *Weltanschauung,* for the warring parties to have recognized a mutuality of interests logically leading to cooperation.[26]

Each market situation would depend, of course, on the concrete degree of approximation to the optimal that various forms of imperfect but vigorous competiton would evince. This is not a question of engaging in measurements of indices of imperfection, trying to gauge departures from hypothetical constructs and supposedly standardized situations of pure competition. It is rather a matter of working out the best possible overall solution. This would include not only the attainment of maxima that are higher than the purely competitive ones for reasons related to the technology of mass production or to consumers' sovereignty, but also the consideration of the whole panoply of direct and indirect economic goals and constraints that Joseph Schumpeter initially, and the literature on economic development more recently, have made us familiar with. This would range the entire spectrum from the promotion of research to a high reinvestment quotient for profits, passing through external economies of all sorts, and including beneficial (desired) cultural effects.[27]

The traditional theoretical economic approach is grounded on the assumption of the existence of a unique model whose functioning is such that, when implemented, the beneficial results of pure competition will correspondingly materialize. Technological characteristics and the market are supposed to coalesce in producing a situation such that the firms' size and number will serve to preclude the possibility of their employing price strategy. In the present context, the utilization of that tactic would be equivalent to competition *with*, which cannot operate in the setting of pure competition, given that interpersonal relations of a conflicting nature are essentially incompatible with it. Purely competitive activity is conducted in a very detached and impersonal manner, each firm being forced by that amorphous entity, the "market" (in reality, the sum effect of all other firms' actions), to conform and behave in accordance with standards and patterns that, from the standpoint of the individual participant, are exogenously generated conditions. Thus, the only kind of competition possible in this environment is competition *for*, which is a form of behavior designed to survive in an inhospitable medium but is not aggression against anyone in particular.

It should be noted, incidentally, that competition *for* as conceived of here is not altruistic or designed to attain nonpersonal or other-directed ends. Nonetheless, it still is a halfway house between economically hostile relations and certain forms of pure cooperation that are implemented through types of action in which each agent individually strives for the attainment of impersonal goals (cooperation *for*, whose purpose is to reach collective goals and to maximize the individual's utility along such lines). Although personal rivalry may still exist in various degrees in these situations, the object toward which the effort is directed cannot be personally appropriated.

It is interesting to notice that, as Schumpeter states, the purely competitive case robs competition of its reality. It is only the stylized and rarefied "limit" case of earthy Marshallian competition. There is little in it of the type of behavior termed *competitive*. Friedrich Hayek has observed, in a similar vein, that the important thing is to study the path that leads to equilibrium rather than the final situation itself.

Competitive Efficiency

There exists an undeniable contrast between the path to, and the ultimate situation of equilibrium, that we find foreign to the normal meaning of the term *competition*.

It is important to keep in mind these transformative processes in the nature of competitive market relations, because in reality they represent, as is implicit in the above observations, partial segments of an entire process of development. One may theoretically start with a classical or neoclassical concept of *actual* or in-process competition and end in a situation characterized by equilibrium of pure competition.[28] Alternatively, subtracting from the latter its perfectionist conditions,[29] we may end up with a variety of no-change market conditions that can be observed in the real world and that have originated in a vast array of different causes, ranging from ignorance and apathy to immobility and lack of financial means. All of these variants, though, share in essence the same genotypic characteristics.

The real world abundantly exhibits, most especially in underdeveloped countries, many nth-best equilibrium situtions, distinguished neither by prevalent in-process and dynamic Marshallian or Hayekian competition, nor by finalistic, stationary-statelike, Chamberlinian market equilibria.

Finally, the diversity of forms of participation and action in a given culture performs the same function relative to the individual that cultural differentiation performs relative to the whole society. In the same manner in which cultural diversity allows for the expression of human values peculiar to, or emphasized by, a given conglomerate of human beings possessed of their own unique antecedents and historical circumstances, we also find that the internal effect of competition provides elbow room for the manifestation of the ultimate existential singularity and essentially monadic character of the human individual, his life, and his experiences.[30]

Let me now inject a simple datum in this current of thought in order to point at some further tentative conclusions. The absolute optimal or *maximum maximorum* position of economic efficiency for plant size, as we can observe in many branches of production in today's developing countries and even in a country such as the United States, may be the medium-sized or large firm, which itself differs greatly from the owner-managed firm or the family enterprise of the past in the nature of intra-firm human relations and degree of participation by those in charge of managerial functions. The transformations brought about by the increasing "democratization" of firms through the capital market and the advent of professional management in the modern world are still by no means logically and historically over. True, the "lone wolves" are gone. The managerial revolution and impersonal administration are in; yet, we have not seen the effects of populism in the ownership of enterprises fully translated into more active and vocal partaking, be it through single individuals or by rival groups' increased participation and assumption of decision-making and supervisory roles in the firm. We really do not know what effects such developments could have on the degree of pure economic efficiency. It is quite possible that changes along these lines will bring about structural mutations in modern-day enterprises. After all, by traveling full circle, we may have the owners (stockholders) back in charge. The demise of the "lone wolves" does not exclude the rule of the many lone wolves.

This is a point that merits a brief comment. The spirit of institutions, as I have already noted, is of the essence of their functioning. Two different institutional morphologies may produce not too dissimilar results or outcomes, as case studies of modern economic development seem strongly to suggest. But also, two similar or homologous morphologies may produce noticeably different results and point at divergent implications because of differences in the anima that characterize them. This observation may be applicable to the comparative study of future participative-individualistic modern enterprises versus group-participative enterprises. The latter type may well tend to appear increasingly in cultural milieus where the relevant unit of organization, decision-making, and behavior is larger than the individual.[31]

The complexity engendered by such potential variations makes it next to impossible to predict what specific mix would correspond to the absolute optimal position obtainable for a given type of production, even under hypothetically unique and strictly determined economic conditions. If the measurement of the degree of monopoly or departure from the "limit" model of pure competition is laden with such difficulties, we can well imagine what would be the case for an abstract comparison among the many possible mixes that would result from combining several different characteristics in alternative organizational models of production. In practice, under static sociocultural conditions, the best approximation we can get to a reasonable degree of economic efficiency will be through the external effect of competition.

It seems appropriate to conclude these thoughts on morphology and efficiency at the level of cultural relativity, which I have used as a frame of reference all along. Obviously, adopting cultural relativity as a premise has served to avoid being led into either of two extreme and improbable positions: (1) that of recommending cultural changes in order to standardize cultures in terms of the values exhibited by one or another of them, or (2) that of speculating about the existence of very specific natural tendencies toward universal uniformity that would assert themselves in time in the historical process of social transformation.

It is very venturesome to speculate as to the general organizational implications contained in any system of philosophy of history. It would be still more conjectural to engage in argumentation pro or contra the merits of standardizing specific and secondary traits in human socioinstitutional life. Still, it seems that the individual man can fully realize his human potentialities within admissible ranges of variation. The important thing, ultimately, is for man to be fully able to exercise his freedom and develop his personality.

It seems to be highly probable, as a matter of fact, that general cultural differences will not disappear in the process of modernization. There is no basis for believing that complete acculturation along Western lines is unavoidable once technological factors are transmitted to, and adopted by, a given culture.[32] Man's potentiality for diversity surely transcends the limits presented by technological constraints and the inflexibilities imposed by production functions. Even the latter are not usually characterized by totally inflexible technical coefficients of production. On the contrary, diversity of production methods and organizational arrangements even allows, as a norm, considerable factor reversal in the ranking of economic activities in different countries.[33] We would also have to consider, of course, the impact of the general spirit of the culture and of the noneconomic institutions and values upon the purely economic organizations of society for a complete appraisal of the possible patterns of interaction and likely direction of cultural change. In this connection it is important to realize the inadequacy of the various brands of economic determinism that see in habitat, technology, and economic structures the independent variables that uniquely determine the values of all other social relations and create their spirit.[34]

Finally, if I may offer a highly impressionistic opinion as to the future unit of control in organizations, decision-making, and behavior in the West, I would advance the contention that the individual will continue to occupy that position. This is not to preclude the possibility that modern societies will partially revert to a more familistic and associational pattern of values and organization. The inner tensions and pressures generated in part by modernity may require these developments as a necessary counterbalance and antidote to them.

Nonetheless, it is unquestionable that the basic philosophical and ethicocultural heritage of the West is built on and around the individual. The relevant unit of value, thought, and action has always, in the Western context, been the individual person. This typically Western mental approach to man and society permeates and invariably influences all aspects of life and culture in occidental nations. It is reflected even in the substance and methodology of the intellectual disciplines and it touches upon the very essence of the message contained in the Christian religion and in Judeo-Christian ethics and morals. It would seem that such foundations are indestructible, short of the cultural annihilation of the Western type of human being and the basic traits of the Western mentality.

Notes

Notes to Chapter 1

1. The "divergence principle" — for which I am sure many applications with varying degrees of gravity could be found, ranging from divination of the strategy of Russia in entering into accommodations with the West to the same type of behavior on the part of a cunning wife — may be stated somewhat as follows: Identical courses of action or behavior modes inspired by different motivations must eventually diverge if their respective goals are to be actualized. If their goal divergence is nonoperational, one might say that from a behavioristic standpoint there are no disparities to take account of.

It can be said that John M. Clark believed in what I have called the "divergence principle." In his *Economic Institutions and Human Welfare* (New York: Alfred A. Knopf, 1961), pp. 207-8, he writes: ". . . and if his [the businessman's] enlightened self-interest is mere farsighted shrewdness, one can be sure that at some point or other the shrewdness will not be farsighted enough and trouble will result." In order to believe that this will not be the case, one would have to assume that interpersonal conflicts arise out of the absence of proper insight into one's true long-run interest. This would amount to a purely formal and definitional solution of the problem. On this point see Gunnar Myrdal, *The Political Element in the Development of Economic Theory* (Cambridge, Mass.: Harvard University Press, 1961), Appendix and p. 240.

2. As Elie Halévy remarks, "For political economy, ever since Adam Smith, has rested entirely on the thesis of the natural identity of interests" (*The Growth of Philosophic Radicalism* [Boston: The Beacon Press, 1955], p. 16).

3. I could define the teleology by paraphrasing Dorothy Emmet, "Function and Purpose" in Nicholas Demerath and Richard Peterson, eds., *System, Change and Conflict* (New York: The Free Press, 1968), pp. 421-24: the unintentional contribution of an agent through his social function to the maintenance of the

complex of activities we call society. On this point see also Joseph Schumpeter, *History of Economic Analysis* (New York: Oxford University Press, 1954), p. 58 n., and especially Friedrich A. Hayek, *Studies in Philosophy, Politics and Economics* (New York: Simon and Schuster, 1969), chap. 6. For a thorough examination of the related idea of the concept of natural law and the existence of a natural social order or set of institutions see Overton H. Taylor, "Economics and the Idea of 'Jus Naturale'", *Economics and Liberalism* (Cambridge, Mass.: Harvard University Press, 1955), pp. 70-99.

4. Economics has, since its modern inception, solved this problem through the theorem of the Maximum Doctrine of Perfect Competition. See Schumpeter, *History of Economic Analysis*, pp. 233-34. This doctrine is founded on the practicing of the competitive rationale by participants, which eventuates, under the assumptions of the model, in a process of unconscious cooperation.

5. By a *Weltanschauung* is meant an apprehension of the world "as is," rather than an ideological preference for what "should be."

6. See Peter Blau and W. Richard Scott, *Formal Organizations* (San Francisco: Chandler Publishing Co., 1962), pp. 5-6, "In every formal organization there arises informal organization." On divergences between organizational and societal values or between societal values and those of administrators, see chap. 1, the introduction by Charles Press and Alan Arian, eds., *Empathy and Ideology: Aspects of Administrative Innovation* (Chicago: Rand McNally, 1966).

7. For an excellent treatment of the sociological and economic shortcomings of this position see respectively: Raymond Aron, *The Industrial Society* (New York: Simon and Schuster, 1968), chap. 3, and James Millar, "On the Merits of the Convergence Hypothesis," *Journal of Economic Issues* 2, no. 1 (March 1968): 60-68.

8. For an interesting article in economics where many related ideas are touched upon, see Peter J. Wiles, "The Political and Social Prerequisites for a Soviet-Type Economy," *Economica* 34 (1967): 1-19.

9. The clash between the classical and the managerial ideology at the corporate level and the emphasis on incomes policy at the macroeconomic level are signs of the changes and needs of the socioeconomic system. R. Joseph Monsen, *Modern American Capitalism* (Boston: Houghton Mifflin Co., 1963), expecially chap. 2, contains a good bibliography on this matter. On the mentioned ideologies, two articles that serve to illustrate the defense of each are: Jack Hirshleifer, "Capitalist Ethics – Tough or Soft?", *The Journal of Law and Economics*, October 1959, pp. 114-19, and Gardiner Means, "The Problems and Prospects of Collective Capitalism," *Journal of Economic Issues*, March 1969, pp. 18-31.

10. See "The Present State of the Debate," published in *Collectivist Economic Planning* (London: Routledge and Kegan, 1935) under his editorship. In this context, it is very interesting to consider, by way of confirmation, which would be the requirements of "perfect computation" in a command economy as described by L. Smolinsky, "What Next in Soviet Planning?", *Journal of Foreign Affairs*, July 1964, p. 607.

11. Competition *for* without competition *with* would not be sufficient to avert inefficiency, the reason being that the absence of the latter forces society

into a narrow range of possible organizational molds of the collectivistic genus.

12. Friedrich Hayek, Ludwig Von Mises, and Milton Friedman are among the most conspicuous representatives of this position. There are, of course, degrees and nuances. In this connection, it is interesting to note that John M. Clark restricts the often-repeated belief that political freedom is *unqualifiedly* dependent on private business.

13. The list of opponents is a lengthy one and includes, of course, many non-Marxists and even nonsocialists. Utopians, Romantics, and Humanists of varying creeds in the history of social and economic ideas would have to be included, along with some modern exponents of Arabian and African socialism. Advocates of "guided democracy" and of nativist and charismatic nationalist movements are candidates for inclusion. The same is true of Christian democratic movements in Latin America and that vast reservoir of vague socioethical feelings catalogued under the misnomer of "Christian Socialism."

It is interesting to note that even Alfred Marshall thought fit to remark that "if competition is contrasted with energetic cooperation in unselfish work for the public good, then even the best forms of competition are relatively evil; while its harsher and meaner forms are hateful" (*Principles of Economics* [London: Macmillan and Co., 1930], pp. 8-9).

14. Sociological conflict theory makes a persuasive case for the integrative function of certain types of conflictive situations. Besides, as has often been remarked in the literature, cooperation does not require consensus or the absence of competition in every sphere of social life. Competitive situations can and do exist normally within larger cooperative or consensual frameworks. Moreover, in the economic context of division of labor, specialization, and social cooperation through the market system, the latter is optimally actualized by means of a competitive mechanism.

15. There is, for example, an optimistic and progressionist view in the late classical and neoclassical school of economists with respect to the melioration of egoistic economic motivations in society. It can be detected in the trilogy of Alfred Marshall, John Stuart Mill, and John M. Keynes's works.

16. See on this point the debate centering on Adolph Lowe's views on the relevance of contemporary economic theory in Robert Heilbroner, *Economic Means and Social Ends* (Englewood Cliffs, N.J.: Prentice-Hall, 1969).

17. For a finely equilibrated example of a substantive and minimal-assumption model of the constituents of human action, see Talcott Parsons et al., "Some Fundamental Categories of the Theory of Action," in Talcott Parsons and Edward Shils, eds., *Toward a General Theory of Action* (New York: Harper & Row, 1962), pp. 3-29.

18. On this point see Melville Herskovits, *Economic Anthropology* (New York: W. W. Norton & Co., 1952), Part 1; Stanley Udy, *Organization of Work* (New Haven, Conn.: Hraf Press, 1959), especially pp. 32 and 117; and Theodore Schultz, *Transforming Traditional Agriculture* (New Haven, Conn.: Yale University Press, 1964), chaps. 1, 2, and 3.

19. Ernest Becker sees the need to explain "man as an *energy-converting and purposive organism* (that)-seeks maximization of his own being, of his own sense

of self," in a survey article, "The Evaded Question: Science and Human Nature," *Commonweal* 89, no. 20 (19): 641. See also Parsons and Shils, *Toward a General Theory*, pp. 14, 18-19.

20. This has been done consistently by political philosophers, philosophers of history, and sociologists. Modern sociology, indeed, is very much interested in the fundamental question of whether or not structure, function, and change can be scientifically integrated in ordered wholes or systems. The nonintellectual, of course, has always been speaking in prose without knowing it. For a very interesting account of Western attempts at synthesizing history and change, see Robert Nisbet, *Social Change and History* (New York: Oxford University Press, 1970).

21. Max Weber and Vilfredo Pareto clearly pioneered in this field before much recent concern with the question arose.

22. The author's position is that man has the potential to develop as a free — nondetermined — being, within the universally admitted limits set by his personal endowments and concrete external conditions. This, admittedly, is to say very little and verges on tautology. Nonetheless, it highlights the purpose of this footnote: to state the belief that deterministic doctrines are inadequate scientific explanations of long-term human behavior and historical development.

23. Man's striving for purpose, integration, and fulfillment carries him in his actions beyond the lucid but mediocre predictability of ends considered by the radical positivist as inhering in the situation itself. Regarding the long pull of history and social action in general as contrasted with utilitarian-inspired immediate and proximate, or routine and habitual actions, German historicism and organicism had a far better point than the theoreticians and model builders have been or are willing to concede. On this point see the fundamental work of Talcott Parsons, *The Structure of Social Action* (New York: The Free Press, 1968), vol. 2.

24. In the Anglo-Saxon tradition this is especially true of work done following the lead of John Stuart Mill. Marshall was very much aware of this development and explicitly recognized the existence of this trend in economics.

25. Erich Fromm in *The Revolution of Hope* (New York: Harper & Row, 1968) brings out this point very clearly. On determining elements in human nature see Clyde Kluckhohn and H. Murray, eds., *Personality in Nature, Society and Culture* (New York: Alfred A. Knopf, 1967), pp. 113-14; Clyde Kluckhohn, "Universal Categories of Culture" in Sol Tax, ed., *Anthropology Today* (Chicago: The University of Chicago Press, 1962), pp. 304-20, and also Bronislaw Malinowski, *A Scientific Theory of Culture* (New York: Oxford University Press, 1960), chaps. 8 to 13.

26. As the collective authors state in Parsons and Shils, eds., *Toward a General Theory*, p. 26, when referring to role types and the differentiation and integration of social systems, "Although the moral consensus of the pattern of value-orientation provides the standards and set the limits which regulate the allocations, there must also be special institutional mechanisms through which the allocative decisions are made and implemented. The institutional roles to which power and prestige are attached play a preponderant part in this process. The reason for this

presuppose an equality of income on the part of the units. All that equality of power really means is that no unit enjoys the capacity to exploit (in the technical economic sense) any other unit.

12. Boulding and Frank H. Knight have elaborated on the thought of the historical extension of the economic realm, or the realm of exchange, in contrast to, and at the expense of, the use of coercion in human relations. Overton H. Taylor expounds on the relations of economy, power and coercion in "Economic Theory, and Certain Non-Economic Elements in Social Life," pp. 117-29. Competition brings about a peaceful leveling of power.

13. On the well-known practical limitations to this hypothetical situation see Frank H. Knight, *The Ethics of Competition* (New York: Harper & Brothers, 1935), especially pp. 47-58.

14. As Boulding has remarked, pure competition really means that there is always an "elsewhere."

15. The question of the size of producing units and its influence upon the individual's maximizing behavior is an interesting one. John Stuart Mill raised it indirectly by his comments on personal efficiency, incentives, and the size of the enterprise, in *Principles of Political Economy* (New York: A. M. Kelley, 1965), pp. 204-5. The two-limit cases for this problem would be: (1) The Guatemalan Indians observed by Sol Tax, *Penny Capitalism* (Chicago: The University of Chicago Press, 1963), who maximize as self-employed individual economic units, and (2) the large modern corporation where, even if pure competition were to exist, maximization would have to take place in an indirect or circumvented fashion through earnings in the factor's market.

16. For a persuasive discussion of this point, see Bert Hoselitz and Wilbert Moore, eds., *Industrialization and Society* (UNESCO: Mouton, 1968), pp. 309-14. Also see Benjamin Ward, *The Socialist Economy* (New York: Random House, 1967), chap. 10, for an apposite account of the difficulties involved in the institution of the workers' councils.

17. Modern managerial research has developed a literary genius along these lines that is all too familiar. Perhaps it should be mentioned in passing that quite a long time before Elton Mayo and Kurt Lewin developed their group approach, Adam Smith (not unlike Erich Fromm nowadays) had called attention to the impact on man of being subjected in his environment to the effects of repetitive situations.

For a highly interesting collection of papers on the experiencing of alienation or anomie and on organizational change provoked by automation, see Simon Marcson, ed., *Automation, Alienation and Anomie* (New York: Harper & Row, 1970).

18. Incidentally, neoclassic economics, in its time, would have been in a much stronger position than we are at present to attack these problems. An interesting starting point for a study of this matter could be Jevons's concept of trading bodies in his theory of exchange (William S. Jevons, *The Theory of Political Economy* [New York: Kelley & Millman, 1957], pp. 88-90). A book by Jerome Rothenberg, *The Measurement of Social Welfare* (Englewood Cliffs, N.J.: Prentice-Hall, 1961), especially chap. 13, contains an excellent analysis of a suggested

lies in the fact that power and prestige possess a highly general significance for the distribution of other facilities and rewards. The distribution of power and prestige and the institutional mechanism which regulate that distribution are therefore especially influential in the working of a social system."

The following quotation is indicative of much of the literature on this point in the context of nonliterate societies: "A man can best satisfy the drive for power and prestige by attaching to himself a group of adherents: to them he affords protection and a lavish board; they give him status and authority. Competition, in a primitive economy, is not specifically economic, but social" (Daryll Forde and Mary Douglas, "Primitive Economics" in George Dalton, ed., *Tribal and Peasant Economies* [Garden City, N.Y.: The Natural History Press], p. 21).

27. The thought-reform technique aiming at the creation of unquestioning, authority-directed individuals is marked by an inevitable side effect: its implementation and the maintenance of desired results require the exertion of a high and widespread level of social coercion and vigilance which, in turn, serve to perpetuate the sharp dichotomy between the policy-making elite and the mass of the people. There is no difference, despite what modern totalitarians like to believe, between "progressive" and "regressive" violence.

28. The general nature of conflict and competition is clearly brought out by the following quotations from Kenneth Boulding: "Conflict is an activity that is found almost everywhere. It is found throughout the biological world, where the conflict both of individuals and of species is an important part of the picture. It is found everywhere in the world of many and all the social sciences study it."

"Conflict may be defined as a situation of competition in which the parties are *aware* of the incompatibility of potential future positions and in which each party *wishes* to occupy a position that is incompatible with the wishes of the other" (*Conflict and Defense* [New York: Harper & Row, 1963], pp. 1, 5). This, incidentally, has nothing to do with the notion of a biologically rooted tendency toward aggression or bellicosity. See Ashley Montagu, ed., *Man and Aggression* (New York: Oxford University Press, 1968), where a contribution by Boulding is found upholding the widely accepted modern view that sees conflict as a "learned" or acquired trait in human behavior and not as a genetic disposition.

29. For a complete investigation of these matters precisely in the light of Christian ethics, see Johannes Messner, *Social Ethics* (St. Louis, Mo.: Herder Book Co., 1949), especially Part 4. Also Herbert Deane, *The Political and Social Ideas of St. Augustine* (New York: Columbia University Press, 1966), pp. 221-43, and Jacques Maritain's elaboration of the scholastic distinction between individuality and personality in his *The Person and the Common Good* (Notre Dame, Ind.: University of Notre Dame Press, 1966).

30. For a modern instance of this see Herbert Marcuse, *An Essay on Liberation* (Boston: Beacon Press, 1969).

31. Even a historically melioristic belief regarding the decreasing role in social life of self-centeredness and self-interest could prove to be quite deceptive. See Arnold Toynbee, *Experiences* (New York: Oxford University Press, 1969), pp. 154-61, and Reinhold Niebuhr, *Moral Man and Immoral Society* (New York: Charles Scribner's Sons, 1960).

Notes to Chapter 2

1. There is, just as in the cooperation-competition dyad, a wide gamut of intermediate positions between pure selflessness and perfect egoism. The following works are an example of how half-way houses, by serving to develop these concepts, have proved very important for the analysis of modern society. David Riesman, *The Lonely Crowd* (New Haven, Conn.: Yale University Press, 1950) and Talcott Parsons, *The Social System* (Glencoe, N.Y.: The Free Press, 1964).
2. See his *The Conflict Society* (New York: Harper & Row, 1966), pp. 257-71.
3. The literature on this last point, which is closely related to the above-referred-to issue of the natural identity and the artificial identification of interests, is covered in Warren Samuels, *The Classical Theory of Economic Policy* (Cleveland, Ohio: World Publishing Co., 1966).
4. This does not necessarily indicate the presence of ill will, but simply of necessity. It is significant to note that economists have never assumed or theorized about the role of coercion and malevolence as a social force. See Kenneth Boulding, *Economics as a Science* (New York: McGraw Hill, 1970), chap. 6.
5. There is no need to elaborate on the literature on this topic. Reference to Milton Friedman, *Capitalism and Freedom* (Chicago: The University of Chicago Press, 1965); Friedrich Haye, *Individualism and Economic Order* (Chicago: The University of Chicago Press, 1948) and *The Road to Serfdom* (Chicago: The University of Chicago Press, 1965), is sufficient to establish the merits of competition in this regard.
6. Notice that this is a shortcoming of the first magnitude insofar as the other-directed utopia is to show some dynamism and is in need of allocating scarce resources to whatever lofty purposes it has decided to attain. Disinterestedness and lack of egoism by no means need lead to a preference for the stationary state, either in technological progress or in the production of goods and services.
7. See Lewis Coser, *The Functions of Social Conflict* (New York: The Free Press, 1969) for a detailed account of the various manifestations of conflict and their effect on social structures. Also refer to n. 14 above. In this connection an article by Ronald Warren, "Toward a Non-Utopian Normative Model of the Community," *American Sociological Review*, April 1970, pp. 219-27, attempts to outline the logic of a harmonization between conflict and social-system theorists in discussing the properties of an optimal sociological and economic model.
8. Incidentally, if there were more than one worldly maximizer, conflict would surely arise among them, given the existence of exchange or distributive relations among these units.
9. On (1) see Louis Schneider, ed., *The Scottish Moralists* (Chicago: The University of Chicago Press, 1967), chaps. 1 and 2, dealing with the uniformity of human nature. Also J. Schumpeter, *History of Economic Analysis*, pp. 121-22, on analytic and normative equalitarianism. In reference to (2) see Hla Myint, *Theories of Welfare Economics* (New York: A. M. Kelley, 1965), especially chap. 12.
10. The program of philosophic radicalism epitomizes this posture.
11. Notice, as is implicit in the text, that an equality of power does not

Notes

socioeconomic approach to the question of individual representation and social choice. For a related reference to cooperative effort and the concept of the primary responsibility of a work-group leader to his men rather than to the employer, see Melville J. Herskovits, "The Problem of Adapting Societies to New Tasks," *The Progress of Underdeveloped Areas*, Bert F. Hoselitz, ed. (Chicago: University of Chicago Press, 1961), pp. 99-101.

19. For typical views and notions on these and related issues in modern welfare economics, a number of works will do, particularly among them, Kenneth Arrow, *Social Choice and Individual Values* (New York: John Wiley & Sons, 1963).

20. This is not to deny, as has been previously noted, the existence for "groups" (in reality for the units composing a group considered collectively) of systemic needs, like collective values, as well as of other structural and functional characteristics, all having a definite economic aspect to them. The economic facet of these needs could be properly considered both as logical prerequisites necessary for the functioning of the economic subsystem in society and as a required explanatory causal element in any attempt at an exhaustive analysis of the creation of actual market values.

Notes to Chapter 3

1. See the reference to John Stuart Mill and John Hicks in Joseph Schumpeter, *History of Economic Analysis*, p. 972 n. A related statement appears in John Kenneth Galbraith, *American Capitalism* (Boston: Houghton Mifflin Co., 1956), pp. 47-49. For a historico-analytic exposition of the maximization concept in the model, see Paul Samuelson, *Foundations of Economic Analysis* (New York: Atheneum, 1965), pp. 203-19.

2. In discussing maximizing conditions, he says: "One aspect of the solution concerns the degree of decentralization in decision-making which is compatible with the maximum conditions. The free market with free individual enterprises offers the well known example of a complete decentralization of production decisions, which is compatible with maximum conditions if the laws of production show decreasing or constant returns and no external effects" (Jan Tinbergen, *Central Planning* [New Haven, Conn.: Yale University Press, 1964], pp. 84-85).

3. See Galbraith, *American Capitalism*, especially chap. 9.

4. The reference here is to short-run price and output behavior. If we were to think of optimality of resource allocation in a more complex and dynamic framework or in a time-extended horizon, Schumpeterian-like solutions favoring oligopoly over more competitive forms would increase in probability.

5. George Stigler has called attention to the practical non-existence of a theory of bilateral oligopoly and takes exception to Galbraith's reasoning and deductions on its possible results. See his "The Economist Plays with Blocs," *American Economic Review*, May 1954, pp. 7-14. The theory of bilateral monopoly, according to Stigler, "offers only contradictions to his theory." He adds: "On the basis of our existing theories, I would expect bilateral oligopoly to be relatively monopolistic in operation" (p. 9). But the next statement seems to me

to have at least a degree of saving power. "It [bilateral oligopoly] would tend more towards competition, the greater the numbers and the easier the entry into both industries...."

6. In Adolph Berle and Gardiner Means, *The Modern Corporation and Private Property* (New York: MacMillan, 1932), the authors long ago commented on the possibility of the interests and motivations of those in control running counter to the interests of the owners (p. 124). The following quotation would nowadays no longer be surprising: "Just what motives are effective today, insofar as control is concerned, must be a matter of conjecture. But it is probable that more could be learned regarding them by studying the motives of an Alexander the Great, seeking new worlds to conquer, than by considering the motives of a petty tradesman of the days of Adam Smith" (p. 350). Monsen, *Modern American Capitalism*, provides a good bibliography on the topic of the managerial ideology of capitalism. The author says on pp. 26-27, "Additionally, the focus of the managerial theme is upon the organization rather than upon the whole competitive system. The organization is a social system in itself; workers, customers, stockholders, suppliers are all part of the organization, a change from the classical version which places the emphasis upon the owner as risk-taker, manager, and creater of the productive forces within the economy as a whole. The managerial theme stresses that the manager is a professional man who has been trained to coordinate and mediate among the various interest groups (without placing the owner's interest above that of any other group)."

7. Experiments in socialist syndicalism have not been historically successful. Although there are many reasons for this, the ones cited in the text have always been present.

Regarding the Workers Councils institution in Yugoslavia, there seems to be considerable doubt as to the actual amount of power they wield. There is no question though that even legally the exercise of their faculties is carefully hedged by the power of other institutions. See chap. 2, n. 16, above, on this point.

8. See Kenneth Boulding, *The Organizational Revolution* (New York: Harper, 1953), pp. xxxii-xxxiv. "The universality of hierarchy in organizations of any size above the very smallest and most informal indicates that it arises out of some deep necessity. This necessity seems to lie mainly in the nature of a communication system (p. xxxii). See his "iron law of hierarchy" (p. 77).

9. Taylorism would be an extreme example of this. See Reinhard Bendix, *Work and Authority in Industry* (New York: Harper, 1956), for a detailed study of the ideologies of management that serve to explain the necessity for the organizational trait of hierarchization and subordination in production. This book confines itself to the study of this phenomenon in the course of industrialization in the West.

10. There are, of course, a multitude of facets to the quest for efficiency in productive organizations. The complexity of the modern literature on organizational and behavioral theory attests to this. The centralization vs. decentralization arguments and the concern of the psychological and human-relations approaches with participation as opposed to more classical or functional views or organization are current examples of some of the points at issue.

Notes

11. See Boulding, *The Organizational Revolution*, for a penetrating analysis of the problems of size of organization, efficiency, and types of human relations. From the more limited viewpoint of the organization of the individual firm, the following article brings up the crucial question of degree of participation and the relationship of this to the quality of the solutions arrived at by this method. Harold J. Leavitt, "Unhuman Organizations," *Readings in Organizational Behavior and Human Performance*, ed. Larry L. Cummings and William E. Scott (Homewood, Ill.: Irwin & Dorsey, 1969), pp. 449-59. The same point is made in the context of the process of economic change by Wilbert Moore, "Industrialization and Social Change," in Hoselitz and Moore, eds., *Industrialization*, p. 313.

12. The study of social change and economic development has brought about the dismissal of crude evolutionary-stage theories and of notions of unidirectional progress, making us much more aware of the importance of cultural diversity in modernization processes. It is now clear that to subscribe to any form of historical or technical determinism would be an extremely naive approach to the challenge of socioeconomic transformation.

13. Peter J. Wiles's discussion in his *The Political Economy of Communism* (Cambridge, Mass.: Harvard University Press, 1962), chap. 1, of various possible ownership models and how their economic effects and likely association with noneconomic variables could differ under varying conditions, is a very interesting instance of this.

14. See Blau and Scott, *Formal Organizations*, pp. 5-6.

15. See Konrad Engelmann, *Building Cooperative Movements in Developing Countries* (New York: F. A. Praeger, 1968), chap. 2.

16. This would be a situation similar to what Peter J. Wiles calls institutional *laissez-faire*. See *The Political Economy of Communism*, pp. 12-18.

17. Max Weber, *The Protestant Ethic and the Spirit of Capitalism*, trans. Talcott Parsons (New York: Charles Scribner's Sons, 1952), p. 68.

18. Richard H. Tawney, *Religion and the Rise of Capitalism* (New York: Harcourt, Brace and Co., 1926), p. 248.

19. Bernard Dempsey, S.J., in "But Don't Call it Capitalism," *Readings in Economics*, ed. Richard E. Mulcahy, S.J. (Westminster, Md.: The Newman Press, 1959), p. 322.

20. See Frederick Nussbaum, *A History of the Economic Institutions of Europe* (New York: Augustus M. Kelley, 1961), chap. 7.

21. For a treatment of this question see "Structure, Conduct and Performance — and Performance, Conduct and Structure?", *Industrial Organization and Economic Development*, ed. Jesse W. Markham and Gustav F. Papanek (Boston: Houghton Mifflin, 1970), pp. 26-37.

22. See Edward Chamberlin, *The Theory of Monopolistic Competition* (Cambridge, Mass.: Harvard University Press, 1956), and William Fellner, *Competition Among the Few* (New York: Alfred A. Knopf, 1949).

23. See Tun Thin, *Theory of Markets* (Cambridge, Mass.: Harvard University Press, 1960), p. 5.

24. William Fellner, *Modern Economic Analysis* (New York: McGraw Hill, 1960), p. 230.

25. Ibid., p. 230.

26. See Kenneth Boulding, *Economic Analysis* (New York: Harper & Row, 1966), vol. 1, esp. pp. 468-75 and 595-99 for a clear analysis of oligopolistic conditions leading to either coexistence or games of survival. Also refer to Phillip W.S. Andrews, *On Competition in Economic Theory* (London: MacMillan and Co., 1964), pp. 49-54, for a discussion of Baumol's noncollusive oligopolistic solution in contrast to that of Fellner.

27. An example of this type of goals and criteria would be the working of the internal effect of competition, which postulates the need for the existence of the alternative options the individual must possess if he is going to effectively enjoy his full political and socioeconomic freedom. Under such conditions, his rights would always be open to exercise rather than constituting a purely formal but unfeasible declaration of principles.

28. As exemplified by Schumpeter in his explanation of the competitive concepts of Marshall, Jevons, Walras, and Cournot. Joseph Schumpeter, *History of Economic Analysis*, pp. 972-75. Marshall's concept of economic freedom and Cournot's concept of unlimited competition could be selected as representative of two polar views on the matter. See Marshall, *Principles of Economics*, pp. 10-11 and Appendix A, on the growth of economic freedom; also Augustin Cournot, *Researches into the Mathematical Principles of the Theory of Wealth* (New York: Augustus M. Kelley, 1960), chap. 8.

29. See Knight, *The Ethics of Competition*, pp. 47-58.

30. In this context it is interesting to observe that Hayek comes out in favor of what Wiles refers to as institutional *laissez-faire*, although only if genuine respect for the preferences of those who do not wish to see their freedom compromised by nonlibertarian schemes is shown. See *Individualism and Economic Order*, p. 127. There is a strong case for the favoring of "happy models" (Wiles). As Wiles comments: "Where the model is compulsory we may be working neither in the most efficient nor in the happiest way. Unless by some chance we all resemble each other *and* the chosen model is the 'best' one for us" (p. 13).

31. This remark applies to a wide gamut of different situations running from the widespread presence of family enterprises in developed France to the existence of the same phenomenon in semi-developed Lebanon and Latin America. It aptly describes the kin-family enterprise in underdeveloped Africa and the paternalism and managerial coopting common in modern Japanese businesses.

32. This topic is amply discussed in the anthropological and sociological literature dealing with this matter. For some well-known instances of this position, see Bert F. Hoselitz, "Interaction between Industrial and Pre-Industrial Stratification Systems," *Social Structure and Mobility in Economic Development*, ed. Neil Smelser and Seymour Lipset (Chicago: Aldine, 1968), and Reinhard Bendix, "Tradition and Modernity Reconsidered," *Comparative Studies in Society and History* 9 (April 1967): 292-346. For a very interesting statement on this question as well as for selective bibliography, see Cyril E. Black, *The Dynamics of Modernization* (New York: Harper & Row, 1967), pp. 194-99. Also refer to Bert F. Hoselitz, "Tradition and Economic Growth," *Tradition, Values, and Socio-Economic Development*, ed. Ralph Braibanti and Joseph J. Spengler (Durham,

N.C.: Duke University Press, 1961) and Bert F. Hoselitz, *Sociological Aspects of Economic Growth* (New York: The Free Press, 1962), chaps. 2 and 3. An article by H. Kishimoto, "Modernization versus Westernization in the East," *Journal of World History* 7 (1963): 871-74, briefly makes the same point. In *From Underdevelopment to Affluence*, ed. Harry Shaffer and Jan Prybyla (New York: Appleton-Century-Crofts, 1968), pp. 67 and 72-73, see excerpts from Robert E. Baldwin and William McCord's writings, where the same position is taken. Concrete instances of technological change and cultural continuity are mentioned by Melville J. Herskovits, "The Problem of Adapting Societies to New Tasks," *The Progress of Underdeveloped Areas*, ed. Bert F. Hoselitz (Chicago: The University of Chicago Press, 1961), pp. 102-12. Morris Opler, in "The Problems of Selective Culture Change" also published in *The Progress of Underdeveloped Areas*, pp. 126-34, makes a strong case against economic determinism: " . . . the use of similar tractors or seed will not necessarily erase the influence of differing backgrounds and traditions" (p. 128), and the likelihood of complete acculturation. "No culture, whatever its new experiences and acquisitions, is likely to become so discontinuous that its present and future will be uninfluenced by its past" (pp.133-34).

33. Perhaps international trade is the branch of economics where, as a matter of practice, this question becomes more evident. So-called factor reversals in different countries for internationally traded goods would confirm the flexibility of technical coefficients. For a discussion of this point, see Hal B. Lary, *Imports of Manufactures from Less Developed Countries* (New York: National Bureau of Economic Research, 1968), chap. 3.

34. See the introduction to *Primitive, Archaic and Modern Economies*, ed. George Dalton (New York: Doubleday, 1968), pp. ix-liv, where the views of Karl Polanyi, who amply researched this question, are expressed. See also on this point, Margaret Meade, ed., *Cooperation and Competition among Primitive Peoples* (Boston: Beacon Press, 1961). For a view critical of the so-called technology theorists' overemphasis on technique as the preponderant factor in modern industrial organization, see Derek S. Pugh, "Modern Organization Theory: A Psychological and Sociological Study," in Cummings and Scott, *Readings in Organizational Behavior and Human Performance*, pp. 34-35.

Bibliography

Andrews, Philip W. S. *On Competition in Economic Theory*. London: MacMillan, 1964.

Aron, R. Raymond. *The Industrial Society*. New York: Simon and Schuster, 1968.

Arrow, Kenneth. *Social Choice and Individual Values*. New York: John Wiley and Sons, 1963.

Becker, Ernest. "The Evaded Question: Science and Human Nature." *Commonwealth* 89: 641.

Bendix, Reinhard. *Work and Authority in Industry*. New York: Harper, 1956.

———. "Tradition and Modernity Reconsidered." *Comparative Studies in Society and History*, April 1967, pp. 292-346.

Berle, Adolph, and Means, G. *The Modern Corporation and Private Property*. New York: MacMillan, 1932.

Black, Cyril E. *The Dynamics of Modernization*. New York: Harper and Row, 1967.

Blau, Peter, and Scott, R. *Formal Organizations*. San Francisco: Chandler Publishing Co., 1962.

Boulding, Kenneth. *Conflict and Defense*. New York: Harper and Row, 1963.

———. *Economic Analysis*. New York: Harper and Row, 1966.

———. *Economics as a Science*. New York: McGraw Hill, 1970.

———. *The Organizational Revolution*. New York: Harper, 1953.

Bibliography

Chamberlin, Edward. *The Theory of Monopolistic Competition.* Cambridge, Mass.: Harvard University Press, 1956.

Clark, John M. *Economic Institutions and Human Welfare.* New York: Alfred A. Knopf, 1961.

Coser, Lewis. *The Functions of Social Conflict.* New York: The Free Press, 1969.

Cournot, Antoine. *Researches into the Mathematical Principles of the Theory of Wealth.* New York: Augustus M. Kelley, 1960.

Dalton, George, ed. *Primitive, Archaic and Modern Economics.* New York: Doubleday, 1968.

Deane, Herbert. *The Political and Social Ideas of St. Augustine.* New York: Columbia University Press, 1966.

Dempsey, Bernard. "But Don't Call it Capitalism." In *Readings in Economics,* edited by Richard Mulcahy. Westminister, Md.: The Newman Press, 1959.

Emmet, Dorothy. "Function and Purpose." In *System, Change and Conflict,* edited by Nicholas Demerath and Richard Peterson. New York: The Free Press, 1968.

Engelmann, Konrad. *Building Cooperative Movements in Developing Countries.* New York: Frederick A. Praeger, 1968.

Fellner, William. *Competition Among the Few.* New York: Alfred A. Knopf, 1949.

———. *Modern Economic Analysis.* New York: McGraw Hill, 1960.

Forde, Daryll, and Douglas, M. "Primitive Economics." In *Tribal and Peasant Economies,* edited by George Dalton. Garden City, N.Y.: The Natural History Press, 1967.

Friedman, Milton. *Capitalism and Freedom.* Chicago: The University of Chicago Press, 1965.

Fromm, Erich. *The Revolution of Hope.* New York: Harper and Row, 1968.

Galbraith, John Kenneth. *American Capitalism.* Boston: Houghton Mifflin Co., 1956.

Halévy, Elie. *The Growth of Philosophic Radicalism.* Boston: The Beacon Press, 1955.

Hayek, Friedrich A. *Studies in Philosophy, Politics and Economics.* New York: Simon and Schuster, 1969.

———. *Individualism and Economic Order.* Chicago: The University of Chicago Press, 1948.

———. *The Road to Serfdom*. Chicago: The University of Chicago Press, 1965.

———. "The Present State of the Debate." In *Collectivist Economic Planning*. London: Routledge and Kegan, 1935.

Heilbroner, Robert. *Economic Means and Social Ends*. Englewood Cliffs, N.J.: Prentice-Hall, 1969.

Herskovits, Melville J. *Economic Anthropology*. New York: W.W. Norton and Co., 1952.

———. "The Problem of Adapting Societies to New Tasks." In *The Progress of Underdeveloped Areas*, edited by Bert Hoselitz. Chicago: The University of Chicago Press, 1961.

Hirshleifer, Jack. "Capitalist Ethics — Tough or Soft?" *The Journal of Law and Economics*, October 1959, pp. 114-19.

Hoselitz, Bert F. *Sociological Aspects of Economic Growth*. New York: The Free Press, 1962.

———. "Interaction between Industrial and Pre-Industrial Stratification Systems." In *Social Structure and Mobility in Economic Development*, edited by Neil Smelser and Seymour Lipset. Chicago: Aldine, 1968.

———. "Tradition and Economic Growth." In *Tradition, Values, and Socio-Economic Development*, edited by Ralph Braibanti and Joseph J. Spengler. Durham, N.C.: Duke University Press, 1961.

———. and Moore, W., eds. *Industrialization and Society*. New York: United Nations Economic and Social Council, 1968.

Jevons, William S. *The Theory of Political Economy*. New York: Kelley and Millman, 1957.

Kishimoto, Hideo. "Modernization Versus Westernization in the East." *Journal of World History* 7 (1963): 871-74.

Kluckhohn, Clyde. "Universal Categories of Culture." In *Anthropology Today*, edited by Sol Tax. Chicago: The University of Chicago Press, 1962.

———. and Murray, H., eds. *Personality in Nature, Society and Culture*. New York: Alfred A. Knopf, 1967.

Knight, Frank H. *The Ethics of Competition*. New York: Harper and Brothers, 1935.

Lary, Hal B. *Imports of Manufacturers from Less Developed Countries*. New York: National Bureau of Economic Research, 1968.

Leavitt, Harold J. "Unhuman Organizations." In *Readings in Organi-*

zational Behavior and Human Performance, edited by Larry L. Cummings and William E. Scott. Homewood, Ill.: Irwin and Dorsey, 1969.

Malinowski, Bronislaw. *A Scientific Theory of Culture*. New York: Oxford University Press, 1960.

Marcson, Simon, ed. *Automation, Alienation and Anomie*. New York: Harper and Row, 1970.

Marcuse, Herbert. *An Essay on Liberation*. Boston: Beacon Press, 1969.

Maritain, Jacques. *The Person and the Common Good*. Notre Dame, Ind.: University of Notre Dame Press, 1966.

Markham, Jesse W., and Papanek, Gustav F., eds. "Structure, Conduct and Performance — and Performance, Conduct and Structure?" In *Industrial Organization and Economic Development*. Boston: Houghton Mifflin, 1970.

Marshall, Alfred. *Principles of Economics*. London: MacMillan and Co., 1930.

Meade, Margaret, ed. *Cooperation and Competition among Primitive Peoples*. Boston: Beacon Press, 1961.

Means, Gardiner. "The Problems and Prospects of Collective Capitalism." *Journal of Economic Issues*, March 1969, pp. 18-31.

Messner, Johannes. *Social Ethics*. St. Louis, Mo.: Herder Book Co., 1949.

Mill, John Stuart. *Principles of Political Economy*. New York: Augustus M. Kelley, 1965.

Miller, John. "On the Merits of the Convergence Hypothesis." *Journal of Economic Issues* 2 (1968): 60-68.

Monsen, R. Joseph. *Modern American Capitalism*. Boston: Houghton Mifflin Co., 1963.

Montagu, Ashley, ed. *Man and Aggression*. New York: Oxford University Press, 1968.

Myint, Hla. *Theories of Welfare Economics*. New York: Augustus M. Kelley, 1965.

Myrdal, Gunnar. *The Political Element in The Development of Economic Theory*. Cambridge, Mass.: Harvard University Press, 1961.

Niebuhr, Reinhold. *Moral Man and Immoral Society*. New York: Charles Scribner's Sons, 1960.

Nisbet, Robert. *Social Change and History*. New York: Oxford University Press, 1970.

Nussbaum, Frederick. *A History of the Economic Institutions of Europe.* New York: Augustus M. Kelley, 1961.

Opler, Morris. "The Problems of Selective Culture Change." In *The Progress of Underdeveloped Areas*, edited by Bert F. Hoselitz. Chicago: The University of Chicago Press, 1961.

Parsons, Talcott. *The Conflict Society.* New York: Harper and Row, 1966.

——. *The Social System.* New York: The Free Press, 1964.

——. *The Structure of Social Action.* 2 vols. New York: The Free Press, 1968.

——, and Shils, Edward, eds. "Some Fundamental Categories of the Theory of Action." In *Toward a General Theory of Action.* New York: Harper and Row, 1962.

Press, Charles and Arian, Alan, eds. *Empathy and Ideology: Aspects of Administrative Innovation.* Chicago: Rand McNally, 1966.

Pugh, Derek S. "Modern Organization Theory: A Psychological and Sociological Study." In *Readings in Organizational Behavior and Human Performance*, edited by Larry L. Cummings and William E. Scott. Homewood, Ill.: Irwin and Dorsey, 1969.

Reisman, David. *The Lonely Crowd.* New Haven, Conn.: Yale University Press, 1950.

Rothenberg, Jerome. *The Measurement of Social Welfare.* Englewood Cliffs, N.J.: Prentice-Hall, 1961.

Samuels, Warren. *The Classical Theory of Economic Policy.* Cleveland, Ohio: World Publishing Co., 1966.

Samuelson, Paul. *Foundations of Economic Analysis.* New York: Atheneum, 1965.

Schneider, Louis, ed. *The Scottish Moralists.* Chicago: The University of Chicago Press, 1967.

Schultz, Theodore. *Transforming Traditional Agriculture.* New Haven, Conn.: Yale University Press, 1964.

Schumpeter, Joseph. *History of Economic Analysis.* New York: Oxford University Press, 1954.

Shaffer, Harry, and Prybyla, Jan, eds. *From Underdevelopment to Affluence.* New York: Appleton-Century-Crofts, 1968.

Smolinsky, Leon. "What Next in Soviet Planning?" *Journal of Foreign Affairs*, July 1964, p. 607.

Bibliography

Stigler, George J. "The Economist Plays with Blocs." *American Economic Review*, May 1954, pp. 7-14.

Tawney, Richard H. *Religion and the Rise of Capitalism*. New York: Harcourt, Brace and Co., 1926.

Tax, Sol. *Penny Capitalism*. Chicago: The University of Chicago Press, 1963.

Taylor, Overton H. "Economics and the Idea of 'Jus Naturale.'" In *Economics and Liberalism*. Cambridge, Mass.: Harvard University Press, 1955.

———. "Economic Theory, and Certain Non-Economic Elements in Social Life." In *Economics and Liberalism*. Cambridge, Mass.: Harvard University Press, 1955.

Tun, Thin. *Theory of Markets*. Cambridge, Mass.: Harvard University Press, 1960.

Tinbergen, Jan. *Central Planning*. New Haven, Conn.: Yale University Press, 1964.

Toynbee, Arnold. *Experiences*. New York: Oxford University Press, 1969.

Udy, Stanley. *Organization of Work*. New Haven, Conn.: Hraf Press, 1959.

Ward, Benjamin. *The Socialist Economy*. New York: Random House, 1967.

Warren, Roland. "Toward a Non-Utopian Normative Model of the Community." *American Sociological Review*, April 1970, pp. 219-27.

Weber, Max. *The Protestant Ethic and the Spirit of Capitalism*. Translated by Talcott Parsons. New York: Charles Scribner's Sons, 1952.

Wiles, Peter J. *The Political Economy of Communism*. Cambridge, Mass.: Harvard University Press, 1962.

———. "The Political and Social Prerequisites for a Soviet-Type Economy." *Economica* 34 (1967): 1-19.

Subject Index

Absolutism, 35
Anarchism, 32-33, 42
Authoritarianism, 15
Capitalism, 52
Classical and neoclassical school of economy, 30, 38, 40, 46-47, 63
Coercion, 29, 36
Collectivism, 15, 32-33
   collectivities, 35, 43
   collectivity orientation, 35
   collectivized centralized economy, 25
Competition, 13, 21, 33, 35-36, 48-49, 54, 56-63
   competition *for*, 22-24, 31, 62
   competition *with*, 22-24, 26, 58-59, 62
   competitive traditional economic theory, 47, 61
   convergence of interests, 23
   external effect, 49, 51, 54, 56
   for economic goals, 25
   Hayekian competition, 62-63
   internal effect, 56
   Marshallian competition, 44, 62-63
   maximum doctrine of perfect competition, 63-64
   Smithian competition, 44

Conflict, 62
Cooperation, 19-21, 32-36, 62
   authority and participation in, 51
   as condition of being, 32
   conscious cooperation, 19, 31, 34
   cooperation *for*, 14, 62
   cooperation *with*, 14
   cooperative participative organizations, 52
   cooperatives, 54
   as an ideology, 20
   noncooperation, 35
   unconscious cooperation, 20
Culture patterns, 53-55, 65-67

Dehumanization, 30
Determinism, 54, 66
Division of labor, 39

Efficiency, 14, 37, 47, 50, 52, 54-56, 64-65
   external, 40-41, 45, 49
   internal, 40-41, 45
   maximal economic, 14, 41, 49, 54, 63-64
   maximization of, 15, 35, 38, 41
   sociopolitical and economic minimization, 37

Subject Index

Freedom, 32, 39-41
    free market, 60-61

Goodwill, 19, 34-35

Hedonism, 28
Human nature, 27, 29-32

Idealism, 20-21
Ideology, 28, 37, 58
Individualism, 35-37, 47
    individual freedom, 41-44, 65
    individual maximization, 35-37, 39, 64-65

Liberals, 21

Marxism, 31
Monopoly, 40, 47, 49, 65

Objectivism, 15, 52
Oligopoly, 42, 47, 49, 60-61
Otherliness, 34

Participation, 52-53
Positivism, 14, 27-28
Praxeology, 20-22
Productivity, 25

Religious ideas, 14, 32, 67

Spirit of institutions and organizations, 54, 57-59, 64, 66
Subjectivism, 15, 20, 22

Teleology, 15, 20
Totalitarianism, 31
Traditional theoretical economic approach, 61

Utility, 38, 43

Variability of social and economic institutions, 35, 39, 56-57, 59

Weltanschauung, 20-23, 27-28, 57, 61
Western culture, 53, 55, 66-67

Index of Authors

Andrews, P. S., 78
Arian, A., 69
Aron, R., 69
Arrow, K., 75

Baldwin, R. E., 79
Becker, E., 70
Bendix, R., 76, 78
Bentham, Jeremy, 20
Berle, A., 76
Black, C. E., 78
Blau, P., 69, 77
Boulding, K., 30, 72-74, 76-78
Braibanti, R., 78

Chamberlin, E., 59, 77
Clark, J. M., 30, 64, 68, 70
Coser, L., 73
Cournot, A., 78
Cummings, L., 77, 79

Dalton, G., 34, 42, 72, 79
Deane, H., 72
Demerath, N., 65, 68
Dempsey, B., 52, 58, 77
Douglas, M., 72

Emmet, D., 68
Engelmann, K., 77

Fellner, W., 60, 77, 78
Forde, D., 72
Friedman, M., 67, 70, 73
Fromm, Erich, 30, 71

Galbraith, J. K., 20, 30, 39, 40, 47, 75

Halevy, E., 68
Hayek, F., 43, 62, 69, 70, 73
Heyekian, 63
Heilbroner, R., 70
Herskovits, M., 70, 75, 79
Hicks, J., 75
Hirshleifer, J., 69
Hobbes, Thomas, 35
Hoselitz, B., 74, 75, 77-79
Hume, David, 19

Jevons, W. S., 74, 78
Jung, Carl, 29

Keynes, John Maynard, 26, 36, 70
Kishimoto, H., 79
Kluckhohn, C., 71
Knight, F. H., 30, 43, 74, 78

Lary, H. B., 79
Leavitt, H. J. 77

Index of Authors

Lewin, K., 74
Lipset, S., 78
Locke, John, 35
Lowe, A., 70

McCord, W., 79
Malinowski, B., 71
Mao Tse-tung, 31
Malthus, Thomas Robert, 36
Marcson, S., 74
Marcuse, H., 72
Maritain, J., 72
Markham, J. W., 77
Marshall, A., 67, 70, 71, 78
Marx, Karl, 30, 31
Mayo, E., 74
Meade, Margaret, 79
Means, G., 69, 76
Messner, J., 72
Mill, John Stuart, 46, 70, 71, 74, 75
Miller, J., 69
Mises, Ludwig von, 70
Monsen, R. J., 60, 76
Montagu, A., 32, 72
Moore, W., 74, 77
Mulcahy, R. E., 77
Murray, H., 71
Myint, H., 73
Myrdal, G., 68

Niebuhr, R., 72
Nisbet, R., 71
Nussbaum, F., 77

Opler, M., 79

Papanek, G. F., 77
Pareto, V., 71
Parsons, T., 35, 70, 71, 73
Peterson, R., 68

Polanyi, K., 34, 42, 79
Press, C., 69
Prybyla, J., 79
Pugh, D. S., 79

Riesman, D., 34, 72
Rothenberg, J., 74

Samuels, W., 73
Samuelson, P., 75
Schneider, L., 73
Schultz, T., 70
Schumpeter, J., 43, 61, 62, 69, 73, 75, 78
Scott, W. R., 69, 77, 79
Shaffer, H., 79
Shils, E., 70, 71
Silvert, K., 35
Smelser, N., 78
Smith, A., 44, 46, 68, 74, 76
Smolinsky, L., 69
Sombart, W., 35, 52, 57
Spengler, J. J., 78
Stalin, Joseph, 25
Stigler, G., 47, 75

Tawney, R., 35, 57, 58, 77
Tax, S., 74
Taylor, O. H., 69, 74
Tinbergen, J., 47, 75
Toynbee, A., 58, 72
Tun Thin, 77

Udy, S., 70

Walras, L., 78
Ward, B., 74
Warren, R., 73
Weber, Max, 35, 57, 58, 71, 77
Wiles, P. J., 69, 77, 78